Ch

Make it matter

Creating communications strategies in the non-profit sector

By Joe Barrell

Publisher: Vicky Browning

For Eding and Stanlow

First published in 2014 by
CharityComms

A CIP Catalogue of this book is available from
the British Library

ISBN: 978-0-9928479-0-6

Designed by
www.chandlerbookdesign.co.uk

Printed in Great Britain by
CPI Anthony Rowe, Chippenham, Wiltshire

CONTENTS

Welcome

The aim of this book is to equip communication professionals in non-profit organisations with the tools and knowledge they need to develop strategies that work – and in doing so, help their colleagues understand the vital strategic role communications can play in fulfilling their organisation's mission.

This guide is aimed at communicators who are about to embark upon, or are in the process of, developing a communications strategy. It will be useful for organisations that have large communications departments, as well as small organisations that have few resources and limited capacity.

The content mainly addresses high-level communications strategies, answering the question, 'How will communications help achieve our organisation's aims?'. However, the principles and approaches will also be helpful to people who are developing a channel-level strategy (for example, a digital or publishing strategy) or a communications strategy for a specific project or campaign.

To produce this guide, we have consulted, interviewed and debated with expert practitioners and theorists across a wide range of charities, researching what they do and how it works. When you are developing your own communications strategy, this book will do a lot of the hard work for you by setting out the key decisions you need to make, as well providing a logical and clear process to follow.

Every organisation is different and has its own set of unique challenges and opportunities. This guide is designed to help you understand the process and decisions involved in creating a clear, compelling and effective communications strategy so you can more easily create your own.

How the guide was written and how to use it

This guide was written following a series of one-to-one interviews and group seminars with communications directors for both large and small organisations across a range of causes within the UK not-for-profit sector. As well as saving you time and energy, their experiences and insights into strategy development should make your strategy sharper and more successful. The aim is to produce a guide that didn't simply tell you how to write a communication strategy (there are plenty of those already), but how others have done it and how they navigated the process.

So we have provided some practical step-by-step tools to help you develop your communications strategy, as well as commentary on how to make it happen.

By its nature, this guide is not comprehensive. Your strategy has to be specific and unique to your organisation, so the book combines general principles and universal methods with hypothetical scenarios for a fictitious charity called 'Homes for Youth' that illustrate some of the processes you will need to go through.

The guide also includes 13 case studies, to show how others have done things. They are drawn from some of the most successful communications strategies of the past few years and will offer inspiration and insight into how your peers have grappled with the challenges you will face. Remember: you are not alone!

You won't need to use everything in the guide. As you develop your strategy, you may choose to address some parts rigorously, with commissioned research and broad consultation with colleagues, supporters, service users or policy makers. Other parts you may decide you can deal with quickly and move on. So just dip in and use the bits that are helpful and relevant to you.

Homes for Youth: Introducing our fictional charity

To illustrate the process and help with practical exercises, the examples are based on a fictional charity called Homes for Youth.

Homes for Youth helps vulnerable young people, most of whom are already homeless, by providing night shelters, drop-in healthcare and information and advice on, for example, training and employment. It also campaigns around welfare benefits for young people, housing and family services.

Homes for Youth is a national UK charity with an annual income of £12 million, made up of 50% from local authority grants, 20% from trusts and foundations, and 30% voluntary income (individual giving, legacies and some corporate).

Currently, Homes for Youth is facing cuts in its local authority funding and competing more with other service providers. It needs to increase its voluntary income, the majority of which it expects to come from individual giving.

Benefit cuts are already affecting young people, putting a strain on families and reducing young people's housing options, with the result that more and more are finding themselves on the streets. The need for Homes for Youth's services is increasing but many young people are unaware of their rights and the services available from Homes for Youth and other charities. None of the main political parties are prioritising this situation.

Homes for Youth understands that if it can get young people to access services, both its own and those from other providers, outcomes will be greatly improved.

Through lobbying and popular mobilisation, Homes for Youth is also campaigning for improved provision of affordable housing, with appropriate support for vulnerable young people.

About the author

Joe Barrell is director of The Eden Stanley Group, a communications, campaigning and fundraising agency that works with non-profit organisations, both in the UK and internationally. Before joining Eden Stanley Joe held a number of senior communications roles, including a stint as director of communications at Save the Children from 2005-2010, and a similar period at Shelter before that. He also serves as a trustee at Action for Children, one of the UK's leading children's services providers, where he has board-level oversight of fundraising, communications, campaigns and policy. Joe champions communications as a strategic driver for charities – with the potential to achieve great things for those that embrace it. He speaks regularly on the topic, and acts as a mentor for up-and-coming communications managers in the non-profit sector.

About CharityComms

CharityComms is the professional membership body for UK charity communicators. We improve the standard of communications and champion its role in the sector, representing, supporting, inspiring, connecting and informing our members and the wider charity communications community. Our vision is for effective and inspiring communications to be at the heart of every charity's work for a better world.

Membership of CharityComms gives you access to inspiring and useful content, including books, reports, seminars, exclusive networking events and a host of opportunities for professional development.

CharityComms

Introduction

What is a communications strategy and why does every organisation need one?

Communications. An afterthought. A helpful yet optional extra that tells people about the 'real' work charities do – like service delivery, policy development and so on. Done right, the thinking goes, it's a neat if non-essential accompaniment to the nitty gritty of the day-to-day. A garnish that complements, but does not finally alter, the meat of what a charity really does.

But the most successful charities of all understand that communications is anything but peripheral. They know that when communications is made central to what an organisation is and does, they – and their mission – thrive. They understand that, far from being just the 'story' we wrap around the 'real work', it's a core ingredient that helps determine the work a charity does, and how it goes about achieving change. As one interviewee put it: "We don't communicate just to tell people about the change we've made in the world. We communicate to make change happen."

Communications can effect change directly, for example, by informing beneficiaries and service users about their rights or providing lifesaving information. It can also mobilise popular support and build public pressure for change in policy and practice, drive organisational growth by attracting and keeping new donors and funders, and recruit great new talent to work in your organisation.

So the most effective organisations are those best equipped to engage and inspire others to act. The best communicators understand this. Their insights and skills – an understanding of audiences and the creative and planning skills to communicate effectively with them – mean they can play a pivotal role at organisational level. If they are allowed to.

This is what we mean by making communications matter. Communications that matter are communications that are tangibly, measurably increasing engagement with your audiences, that are making more and more people choose you in some way. Making it matter means making your communications a centrepiece of your organisation – a central strategic function that tells you who you need to influence to achieve your goals, and above all what you want them to think, feel and do.

Making your communications matter, then, is one of the swiftest routes there is to making your organisation matter too.

More than just your organisation's story

A communications strategy isn't just about lifting the lid on your organisation and showing everyone everything it does. It's deciding what to communicate, with whom, to deliver the greatest impact. It's about defining the unique contribution you can make in the world and answering the question 'What can communications do to help our organisation achieve its goals?'.

For these reasons, your communications strategy won't be identical to your organisational strategy. You might choose to turn the volume up on one aspect of your work and focus on a particular segment of your audience. Try this analogy: If you were in the mobile phone business, you wouldn't dedicate 80% of your communications strategy to promoting your engineering work, even though engineering might make up 80% of your business. You would focus on the unique service you provide, your value for money or customer service, because that's how you will sell more phones. It's the same in the non-profit sector. You will need to think about what's going to motivate your audiences to engage with you and how that's going to achieve the change you need. That's not the same as telling the whole story to everyone.

What do we mean by communications?

The term 'communications' is used in this guide to cover any external engagement with audiences through mass communications channels.

This guide doesn't specifically address internal communications, or inter-personal forms of communications such as government relations – although the principles outlined should be relevant in any context.

Most of our attention in this guide will be communications delivered through the four main media channels: bought, earned, social and owned, which are covered in greater depth in the section on channel planning (see Chapter 7).

However, two disciplines overlap within the area of communications: marketing and brand.

Marketing describes the use of a combination of media to promote a product or service where the return on investment is easily defined and measurable. Given that a central tenet of this guide is that all communications should have defined objectives, it's not very useful to draw distinctions between marketing and communications.

Brand relates to managing and building your organisation's reputation and positioning so that people are more predisposed to engage with you in some way. We discuss brand strategy in this guide, thinking about your brand as an influencing mechanism, but other more in-depth publications are available on this topic (see Resources).

Three definitions of communications strategy

From the interviews, there are three definitions of communications strategy that emerge:

- **A means of achieving organisational objectives**. Zoe Amar, former head of marketing and business development at LASA and now a marketing and digital communications consultant, says: "It's about deciding where you want to go and how you are going to get there, then using communications to achieve it. For example, if the business strategy wants to increase training turnover by 10%, my communications strategy will look at ways to do that."

- **Primarily about positioning.** For Daniel Dodd of the National Trust, this means, "Having a bigger voice for the National Trust and communicating 'Love of Special Places'." Meanwhile, Mathurot Chuladul from Making Music says: "From the strategy, we figure out what we want to be known for and what we want our members to know."

• **An articulation of 'how we do things'.** Or as Claudine Snape from Asthma UK says: "An organisational framework for what, where, why, how and to whom we communicate."

All three definitions are helpful because they explain a) what we want to achieve, b) how we want to be positioned, and c) how we're going to make it happen.

When contributors were asked to describe the common characteristics of effective communications strategies, three themes emerged.

1. **Strong alignment with core business aims.** This implies communications objectives that link to organisational objectives, with a clear strategic purpose.

2. **An approach to meeting your organisation's unique challenges**. While there are some universal approaches, it's important that it's your strategy that explains your communication challenges and how you will tackle them. This indicates a strong understanding of the external environment you are operating in.

3. **An enabling and guiding framework**. Your strategy needs to be useful and something that guides your work, without being too prescriptive. It should be easily explained and its value well understood.

The difference between a strategy and a plan

A communications strategy is not the same as a communications plan. It focuses on the big picture, explains what your organisation wants to achieve through communications, and gives a rationale for that achievement. It gives you the 'what', 'why' and 'with who'. Meanwhile, a communications plan focuses on 'how' and 'when': in other words, how you will implement your strategy and your schedule of activity. Still, a strategy without a plan isn't going to be much use, and later on we suggest a process for developing the 'big tactics' that will help turn your ideas into action and get your strategy off the page and into the real world.

Simple and memorable

Ultimately, a strategy needs to be simple. The process of developing it can sometimes feel stodgy and complex, and usually means grappling with some difficult questions. But the final output should be clear and straightforward. Remember why you are developing your strategy and who it's for. The clearer the strategy and the easier it is to understand, the more people – inside and outside the organisation – you will take with you. It's tougher to write a short one than a long one, but that's what you should aim for. And it needs to be memorable, because nobody's going to keep it open on their desk to refer to every day – or even once a week.

How long should your strategy run for?

When we put this question to our communications heads, most thought that three years was about right. Most agreed that one year is not enough to achieve big strategic objectives, and that five years is too long to be able to make reliable predictions about the challenges your organisation will face and the tools you will have to meet them – particularly given the fast pace of change in digital communications. Whatever shelf life you decide on, you should plan for a yearly review, to check progress and make any necessary adjustments, update your key messages, and so on.

Think creatively

This guide describes a staged process, including methods and exercises for developing your strategy. But it's important to say up front that the process alone won't give you the answers you need. The answers will come from you and your colleagues. The process you go through is simply a way of exposing you to the right information at the right time to make good decisions.

Strategy development is not painting by numbers. It's a creative and thoughtful process, and the aim of this guide is to provide the stimuli to make yours as good as it can possibly be.

A communications strategy is a framework within which the whole organisation can develop its communications so that the impact of those communications is maximised. It also helps make decisions on where to put most of our effort, creative thinking, staff time and budget. It answers what we will have achieved if we have succeeded.

"It's more than just about messaging and channels for the communications team; for it to be successful it needs to be owned and understood by the whole organisation. Achieving that ownership is a challenge. We campaign, and campaigning is about communicating so it's important that people understand what a communication strategy can do for them.

"At times in our history we've been very much a service function, but when we've had a strategy we've become more of a strategic driver in the organisation, and that's how we're now viewed: as a strategic function.

Adeela Warley, Friends of the Earth

Developing an international communications strategy

The examples and case studies in this guide all relate to national UK non-profits. So what's different if you are developing a communications strategy for an international charity?

Much of what you need to do will be the same, but you will have to decide what you can do centrally and what needs to be done by your organisation's national or country offices. It could be the role of international headquarters to develop a brand strategy and broad communications aims, but it's unlikely that you will be able to carry out research directly with audiences in your programme countries. So you won't be able to develop the same level of detail or a strategy that fits all countries and contexts.

National offices will likely have much greater in-depth knowledge of national audiences, including which media they are using, what's culturally appropriate, and whether there are any political sensitivities. You will need to listen to what country directors and communications specialists have to say about the context they are working in, but you shouldn't be reticent about stressing the power of good communications and their ability to bring about change.

Countries primarily concerned with programme delivery may need convincing of the need for a strong brand and powerful communications – for example, by demonstrating their importance in attracting and maintaining funding. They might also have their own need for specific communications aimed at, for example, changing behaviour, increasing the reach and impact of their programmes, and political influencing.

Head office communications teams can act in a support and advisory capacity, providing guidelines, tools and resources for national strategies and plans. They can also advise about what resources national teams will need in terms of skilled staff and communications equipment and software, and provide training and investment if necessary.

It's a two-way process, because international charities also need resources and content (such as film, photos and case studies) from country programmes. For humanitarian agencies, staff in field offices are increasingly providing content directly through blogs, tweets or video. And communications aimed at UK audiences now reach international audiences, making a consistent brand and coherent messages all the more important.

We've designed templates for how to develop communications strategies and plans, as well as workshop plans to help country programmes develop their strategies. We've just begun to have a consistent process for business planning, and this has enabled better processes for communications strategy planning too.

Helen Marsden, Marie Stopes International

1

Getting started and who to involve

Strategy can sound abstract and opaque, something non-specific that's easy to fudge. Indeed, the temptation is to throw away the books, whip out a laptop and hammer something out there and then. After all, how hard can it be?

That kind of energy is no bad thing – after all, you have to start somewhere. But your strategy, if you get it right, will set your course for the next few years, and is not something to take lightly. There has to be a structure and a plan of attack, so plotting that out is a good place to start.

The seven stages of strategy development

You will need to go through a number of stages to develop your strategy, which we'll look at briefly now:

1. **Discovery phase: review and benchmark**
    Take stock of where you are in terms of your external operating environment, your performance to date, and your existing capacities. This should provide you with material to guide all of the subsequent stages so don't skip it.

2. **Agreeing and setting objectives**
    Look at your organisation's objectives and figure out where and how your communications function can achieve the greatest impact. Then translate this into coherent, measurable communications objectives.

3. **Defining your audiences**
   Decide who you are talking to, and understand what makes them tick. Then work out what you want them to think, feel and do. This will inform how you position your organisation and which channels and messages will engage your audience.

4. **Setting brand goals**
   Understand and articulate the role of your brand in achieving your communications objectives. Likewise, decide how your communication strategy will build engagement with your organisation and, critically, who your brand is for.

5. **Message development**
   Develop your core script, showing what you need to say about your organisation and your issues. This will help keep your colleagues on message and deliver coherent and purposeful communications.

6. **Channel planning**
   Consider which channels will reach your audiences and which skills you need in your team. You should also consider the 'Big Tactics' to use to achieve your strategic aims (see Chapter 7).

7. **Making the case for investment**
   You will need to persuade your board or executive team that your strategy is going to achieve impact for your organisation and is worth spending money on.

There's no one-size-fits-all approach, but you will have to consider all seven stages to some extent. And you don't necessarily need to follow the process in the same order. Given the day-to-day reality of working in a non-profit organisation, you may find other factors mean you have to do things differently. For example, your planning cycle may demand that you bid for investment before you are quite sure how you will spend it.

Starting up

A good first step to developing an effective strategy is taking the time to read as much as you can on the subject – including this book. Once you have decided on the strategy development process that's going to work for you, it will be useful to write it up, with a simple timeline, to show colleagues what you are planning to do, over what period, and how they can join in.

You may also find it useful at this stage to produce a skeleton draft of your strategy (see p149). This is a short document giving an outline of what you expect the final strategy to cover. It comprises a list of the main headlines and short 'scope notes', detailing in a few sentences what each section will address. You could base this on the seven stages we go through in this guide. Sharing a skeleton draft with your colleagues is a simple way of explaining the process you are embarking upon, and inviting their feedback can help you get their agreement that the project is needed and your approach is right.

You will also need to decide who to involve, both in your project management team and for wider consultation. We've gone into a little more depth on that in the next section. Then compile all of these elements – a process and timeline, skeleton draft and terms of reference for the project management team – into a single project plan to share with your organisation.

Who to involve

If it's a good one, your strategy is likely to result in change, and there will be people in your organisation you will need to help achieve it, just as there will be people who will resist. So before you dive into the strategy development stages, you need to think about who has to be involved from the start. If your strategy is to become the enabling and guiding framework you want it to be – if it's to be a useful tool that's adopted by the organisation and invested in – you need people in your organisation to be aware of it, understand it, believe in its value and want to be part of it.

You will need to build engagement across the organisation – with your team, senior management and key people in other departments – for two reasons:

1. You need colleagues to recognise the strategic role communications plays in achieving organisational aims.

2. You need to bring people on board, to help you develop and implement the strategy.

This cannot be overstated: success or failure in bringing and keeping the right people on board will determine the success or failure of your strategy – it's that simple. Bringing them in at the end, as you unveil your beautifully crafted, ground-breaking strategy, may be too late and your hard work will be lost.

 The people and the process matter more than the final document. If you haven't brought people with you, it doesn't matter what the final document says.

Selena Chapman, Marie Curie

Don't use your communications strategy to persuade directors to invest in it. That's the wrong way round – you will just send them to sleep and they won't buy into it. If communications isn't an organisational priority for the CEO and senior leaders in the first place, you won't get anywhere. You need them to co-create and find the insights with you. Facilitating the right process can help people understand that communications is 'how change happens' rather than just thinking about 'the story of the organisation'. This will not only build consensus but will also ensure some big steps are taken and your organisation will move forward together.

Ben Hewitt, Save the Children International

EXERCISE 1:
Stakeholder analysis matrix

Begin by mapping who you need to involve, why you need to involve them, and how crucial their support is to the success or failure of your strategy. The example overleaf shows a standard stakeholder matrix, which is a simple tool to help you with this. It has two axes: Power and Interest, marked High to Low.

Try mapping your colleagues. Where would you place them? Your boss is likely to be in the top right, as they have the power to approve your work and a very real, personal interest in making sure it meets their expectations. Your board will be in one of the top two quadrants, but more likely on the left, depending on how engaged they are with communications. Bottom left are the people in your organisation that don't think much about communications and probably don't matter too much at the moment (although you might want to mobilise them, so don't forget about them altogether). Finally, bottom right will be those colleagues who are on-side and see the need for the work you are doing but are relying on you to make it happen.

Once you have done this mapping exercise, it should help you throughout the process when considering who to inform and who to involve. Think about:

- Who will bring knowledge and insight to provide content and help me make the right decisions?

- Who do I need to help me implement this, in both developing and rolling out the strategy?

- Who controls the resources – people, money, time – that I need to make this happen?

- Who are my champions, who will persuade others that this is the big show in town?

Then tell them you are going to develop a communications strategy and that you want them all to be involved.

EXAMPLE: Stakeholder analysis matrix

High	**MEET THEIR NEEDS**	**MANAGE CLOSELY**
	Engage and consult on areas of interest	The reaction of key players towards the project must be a first consideration. Involve in governance and key decisions, and engage and consult them regularly
POWER	**MONITOR**	**KEEP INFORMED**
	Inform via general communications: newsletters, website. Monitor carefully in case their position in the matrix changes. Try to engage them	Keep informed and consult on interest areas. Potential supporter/goodwill ambassador
Low	**INTEREST**	High

The most important thing is having a shared vision at the start. You need a process where the senior leadership is involved in understanding the importance and value of a good communications strategy and the impact it will have.

You need to bring all functions together – not just the usual suspects, but HR, finance and other support functions – and ask them to be really honest about their expectations. Try a meeting where you diagnose your challenges together – and build consensus on what your strategy needs to achieve. There's an exercise I use where I break a meeting into groups and ask people to come up with a newspaper article from three years in the future. Where would they like to get to? Something even this simple can help you start to build that shared vision. Once you've discussed all their ideas you will find there is a much greater understanding of what communications is about – and your role in moving the organisation forward.

Ben Hewitt, Save the Children International

Asserting the strategic role of communications

For many charity communicators, one of the toughest challenges they face is getting colleagues to understand and recognise the strategic role of communications.

This challenge can be compounded by internal culture, particularly when a charity's management is dominated by programme experts, fundraisers or policy staff, each of whom may bring very different perspectives to the role of communications. Moreover, some communicators admit they lack confidence in talking strategy. And why wouldn't they? The career path of successful communicators is typically through media relations, brand development or digital communications, so the peculiar MBA-speak often heard at executive level can seem opaque.

So how do you get past this and assert the strategic role of communications in your organisation? The best way is to have a written communications strategy in the first place, involving your colleagues in the process. But that alone may not solve the problem. It can take patience and some careful navigation, particularly if your communications department is structurally below the top level of senior management. Here are some things you can try:

What's in your tool box?

Think about what knowledge and information you and your team uniquely bring to the table. It's likely that your unique contribution is an insight into the external environment – what people outside think and know about your organisation and your issues. So your tool box might include snapshots of media coverage by issue, latest audience research, channel performance (eg media and digital traffic), brand performance, competitor activity, and so on. If you can, compile this information into quarterly reports (or at the very least, have it ready at the start of your organisation's planning and budgeting cycle) then develop and share a narrative for what this information is telling you and its implications for your organisation. Your role could be keeping your senior management team focused on the external environment, which is a healthy place to be.

How does your team benefit the organisation?

When you describe the work of your communications team, frame it in terms of the charitable aims it achieves and the benefits it brings to the organisation, as opposed to narrowly defined communications outcomes. For example, instead of "We're raising awareness of breast cancer" ("So what?"), try "We're inspiring people to take action on breast cancer" ("OK, I see the contribution you are making!"). Try to do this in your everyday conversations, but also consider more systematic ways of promoting the impact your team makes, such as strengthening your presence in staff inductions, creating a 'year book' highlighting your team's achievements, or attending team meetings in other departments to showcase your team's work.

Who will be your internal ambassadors?

Strengthen your relationships with colleagues in other departments and recruit ambassadors or 'champions' for strategic communications. This is particularly important if communications is not a senior management function, as you will need strong advocates at executive level.

How will you take the lead?

Establish your team in a convening role by putting together multi-disciplinary project teams from across the organisation to work on communications initiatives, and take the lead in delivering projects. You are a communicator, so you are good at planning, right? Use these skills to assert the strategic role of communications in your organisation and persuade and convince others to come on board.

Recently, we've established some multidisciplinary teams to work on major projects – usually a campaign. We assign a major campaign coordinator who makes sure there is a plan with a critical path, milestones and so on. They organise a core group of people from other teams who create the campaign with the support of a 'delivery team'. This mechanism means the communications department is seen as creating the campaign, rather than being a service function, and has helped put communications planning at the heart of campaign development, where it should be.

Adeela Warley, Friends of the Earth

CASE STUDY: British Heart Foundation: Communications at our core

Tamara Bennett, senior media manager and
Nick Radmore, head of social marketing and
brand, British Heart Foundation (BHF)

As the nation's heart charity, communications is central
to the British Heart Foundation's mission to fight heart
disease. Our communications activity has prompted people
to change behaviour to improve their health, undertake
superhuman feats to fundraise, and lobby influencers to
affect change. During 2012 - 2013 we carried out research
to understand how the public connects with our cause. This
resulted in a new approach for the BHF which helped place
communications activities at the heart of our strategy.

Our challenge

One of our key challenges was perception of our cause. Last
year we set about a project looking at how to tell the BHF
story in a way that truly resonated with our supporters and
put heart research at the centre of our activities. We called
this our 'Fight for Every Heartbeat'. This communications
strategy helped set the tone for our new five-year
organisational strategy which came into force in 2014.

Our journey

Communications are key to telling our story. We needed to
move the charity to face in the same direction with a single-
minded focus. We involved teams across the organisation
and worked together to:

- Craft a new narrative about heart and circulatory disease
  based on robust research with our supporters and key
  stakeholders

- Define our centre of gravity and research what truly
  resonates with the 2.3 million people living with heart
  disease across the UK

- Radically simplify the way we present the BHF and our core
  activities

- Ensure internal clarity on BHF's role and reason for being

- Learn more about perceptions, attitudes and
  giving behaviour

- Agree the priorities for change as an organisation.

Activating our Fight for Every Heartbeat

We wanted to put our Fight for Every Heartbeat at the core of every communication. Our aim was clear - we needed to position the BHF as a charity with a relentless determination to succeed by:

- Increasing the relevance and understanding of heart disease among the general public and raise awareness that it can affect anyone and everyone

- Increasing propensity to support the BHF.

Fewer, bigger, better

Our research showed that we needed to implement a clear communications strategy to help the public engage with our vision and donate to our cause. A few simple changes made a big difference:

Hero campaigns: We moved from a position of doing several major campaigns each year to four 'hero' campaigns. This helped define our focus externally and internally. This streamlined approach allowed us to focus our messaging and energies on the 'big moments' throughout the year.

Every hero campaign is linked directly to our organisational strategy with research underpinning every campaign creative. We believe it's essential for all of our communications activities to align with our organisational objectives.

Communications calendar: We developed a communications calendar which outlined a month-by-month focus for the organisation. The hero campaigns were included alongside smaller key projects which needed support and promotion.

An integrated approach: We work to deliver holistic, integrated communications that support the charity's work by creating content and managing relationships across digital and traditional channels in a seamless manner. A number of agencies are involved in hero campaigns including digital, advertising and fundraising agencies. Instead of briefing them separately, we brief them as one agency for hero campaigns and challenge them to work together on a solution for the campaigns – what we call a 'loop team'. We also created a cross-charity group to help drive our Fight for Every Heartbeat. This integrated approach helps 'sell' communications as a vital ingredient of any project or campaign.

Sustaining momentum

We knew that increasing understanding of and sustaining Fight for Every Heartbeat wouldn't happen overnight. Through hard work, determination and client management skills we make every effort to ensure colleagues understand and recognise the strategic role of communications on a daily basis.

The following tactics have helped raise the profile of communications across the organisation:

Client service: The communications division works with teams across the organisation to develop briefs and plans to meet their aims and objectives for projects and campaigns. Regular meetings help us develop strong working relationships across the charity.

Brief, plan, evaluate: Fully-integrated plans across PR, digital and marketing help us deliver a 360 degree approach to communicating our cause. We also involve a number of teams in idea generation and planning. We have a strong focus on evaluation and include a range of analytics from social engagement to volume of media coverage which help demonstrate the difference communications can make.

Clear results: Above all else we aim to get results. From increasing donations to our BHF shops to generating petition signatures, we are able to clearly demonstrate the impact communications has in helping to achieve the charity's mission and vision.

Bravery: We are a brave communications department and we're willing to take a risk to create a buzz around the work of the BHF. For example last year we staged a virtual hijack of cigarette packets using Blippr technology. Our Vinnie Jones 'Hard and Fast' campaign has saved over 40 lives to date. These are just two examples of the way we innovate to help communicate our life-saving messages to our supporters.

Action points
from Chapter 1

- Take time to decide on the stages you need to go through – and in which order.

- Draw up a project plan – including a simple timeline and terms of reference – and share it with the people you need on board.

- Create a project team (or teams) and enlist communications champions throughout the organisation.

- Start asserting your strategic role right away, and decide how best to achieve that.

2

Discovery phase: review and benchmark

You can't begin any journey without first taking stock of your surroundings – if only to be sure you don't end up in the same place you started out from. Happily for us, we won't need a compass or an in-depth knowledge of astronomy to do it, just a willingness to ask the right questions and listen objectively to the answers.

So before embarking on developing your strategy, you need to look around you and find out where you are. This will help you to:

- Understand your operating environment and identify your main challenges

- Assess your existing capacities and performance to date

- Provide a baseline or benchmark for objective setting and longer-term tracking of your strategy

- Further engage your colleagues in the strategy development process

- Develop insights and inspiration for your future direction.

This process can be as extensive or as light-touch as you see fit, depending on your resources and how much time you have. But you will need some information and insight to inform your thinking, so don't skip this phase. Communications strategies that aren't informed by a real understanding of the external environment are of little or no use.

At a minimum, you should conduct three pieces of analysis: a

PEST, SWOT and a competitor audit. They will give you the big picture of what's happening around you and your readiness to take on your challenges, as well as set the context for your strategy and anchor your thinking in the real world. Further activity used to gain deeper insights is covered later.

Some of this you can do on your own or with your team, but you should also look outside your organisation for insight. You could talk to experts in your sector about current trends and the opportunities for your organisation, or to your media contacts about how you might build stories about your issues.

This stage of your strategy development process is all about discovery, and it can be enlightening and full of surprises. We've provided some exercises here to help you structure your research and organise the results. They will all help you to build up a picture of where you are and start you on the journey to where you want to be.

For our previous communications strategy in 2010, we went through a PEST analysis and a competitor review. Our agency did a lot of in-depth interviews with staff, the board and local group members, and that helped us distil the issues our strategy needed to work on. There are a lot of people with strong views about what the organisation is about, with some inevitable tensions, which needed to be aired and resolved. This helped us get a lot of 'buy-in', including from the board and senior management team.

Adeela Warley, Friends of the Earth

EXERCISE 2:
PEST analysis: what's happening in the world?

A PEST (political, economic, social and technological) analysis is a great way to start things off. Your colleagues may have already done one, in which case you can build from it to look at specific communications challenges. Your PEST analysis will give you a narrative to underpin and guide your strategy, answering the following key questions:

- What are your organisation's **political** challenges? For example, how will existing and proposed legislation impact on your beneficiaries or campaigning environment?

- What are your **economic** challenges, especially in relation to your funding streams – both statutory and voluntary?

- What **social** issues or societal shifts will you have to contend with, both in terms of your beneficiaries and the attitudes of your supporters?

- How is **technology** affecting your organisation or your beneficiaries, and what opportunities does it bring? In the context of a communications strategy, this question could address how it has impacted on the media and how your audiences behave.

Here's an example created for our fictional charity, Homes for Youth.

PEST – Homes for Youth

Political

- Government is focused on meeting education targets and social care investment is declining

- No long-term government strategy on young people's homelessness, and youth homelessness is not in main party manifestos

- There seems to be growing media interest in social exclusion of young people, linked to narrowing housing options

Economic

- Local authority spending cuts are likely to squeeze statutory funding

- Greater competition from the private sector in outsourced service provision

- Young people's benefit cuts are forcing more onto the streets

Social

- Family breakdown is on the increase.

- There is an upward trend in health problems such as TB and STIs in young people

- The public may be less sympathetic to excluded young people following recent unrest

Technological

- Social media through mobile phones is increasingly a lifeline for those homeless young people who can access it

- Online giving and campaigning is up across the sector and there are untapped opportunities to engage with potential supporters

EXERCISE 3:
SWOT analysis: how are we doing internally?

To understand as much as possible about your existing capabilities, and make sure the strategy builds on your strengths and is rooted in the reality of what can be achieved, you should conduct a SWOT analysis, which looks at strengths, weaknesses, opportunities and threats.

While SWOT isn't just about looking internally (opportunities and threats are external too), the aim is to focus on how ready you or your team are to deliver a strong communications function. Work with your team (if you have one) to build a shared understanding about what is and isn't working, and start to come up with early ideas about where your strategy could take you.

Also include a creative review of your communications materials. Do they hang well together? Do they convey your brand effectively? What impression do they give and what, in totality, are they saying? Also talk to internal colleagues to get their views of your team's role and performance, and use structured interviews that can be repeated a year later to see how far you've progressed.

Here's our Homes for Youth SWOT.

SWOT example – Homes for Youth	
Strengths • Homes for Youth has a long history and good reputation • We have good links with several MPs in main parties • Our financial supporters are loyal – once they're in, they tend to stay with us	**Weaknesses** • We're seen as London-based rather than as a national charity • Our brand is perceived as old-fashioned • Lack of coherence between communications from different departments
Opportunities • The board and senior management are keen to develop communications • Upcoming general election may give greater media visibility to our issues • Some new corporate partnerships may give us access to new market segments	**Threats** • We're behind the curve on digital communications • We're expecting a difficult budget round, and so we may have to curtail our ambition • We've never had a communications strategy before, and our colleagues may not see the value of what we're doing

Your competitors

In the non-profit sector, we can be shy about referring to similar organisations as 'competitors'. After all, we're all working towards similar goals and we should collaborate whenever we can. Nonetheless, there will be other organisations working in your field that you work with both as partners and as rivals, and there's nothing wrong with that. The creative tension that brings is part of what keeps the sector in good health. In this initial discovery stage, we recommend that you think about who these organisations are and define your competitor set. These are the organisations you will learn from, measure yourself against, and try to differentiate yourself from. Your strategy process should begin with getting to know them better.

Here are some things you should try:

- Create a list of your key competitors – around five – including where possible organisations both larger and smaller than yours.

- See if they will meet and talk with you. Nobody's going to give all their secrets away, but the better you know each other, the more effective you will be.

- Look at their websites, marketing material, press releases and annual reports to get a picture of what they are talking about and how they are positioning themselves.

- Get hold of quantitative data if you can, because it will help you measure up and give you tools to track progress over time. This might include brand performance (awareness or preference), media performance, media spend, digital performance (including website traffic and social media activity) and so on. As well as comparing your performance, tracking your competitors might also reveal more general trends that affect your whole sector. See the section on channel planning for some low-cost sources for this data.

- Consider what you can learn from this data. Play with it and see what happens. What's the relationship between brand strength and voluntary income in your sector? Does social media correlate with website traffic? Who's performing best in the regional, broadsheet or popular press – and what seems to be the effect of that?

It's all too much!

At the early stages of strategy development you may feel a little overwhelmed with information and your task can suddenly seem more complicated than it was when you started. But hang on in there – this discovery will prove invaluable in developing your strategy. It will anchor your processes in the real world and some big themes will quickly emerge to inform your thinking and decision making as you progress.

Remember – don't be enslaved by this process. We're just trying to immerse you in the right information to help you have some good ideas and make some good decisions.

Action points from Chapter 2

- Do your research. The more you find out now, the better your strategy will be and the more money and time you will save later.

- Carry out a PEST analysis so you know what's happening in the world around you and what your challenges might be.

- Find out how effectively you're responding to these challenges, and consider how you might improve, by doing a SWOT analysis.

- Get to know your competitors – what can you learn from them and how are you performing in comparison?

3

Setting objectives

Strategic communications are all about helping your organisation achieve its aims. Organisational priorities are key and anything achieved by your communications should be measured against organisational goals rather than their own ends.

Your communications objectives therefore need to be closely aligned with your organisation's aims. You will need to begin with the question, "What is this organisation trying to achieve?" then "What can communications do to help achieve it?".

> When I joined Anthony Nolan, I felt there was a disconnect between the organisational strategy and individual plans. We've refreshed this and now it's clear how each communications objective relates to organisational aims.
>
> **Richard Davidson, Anthony Nolan**

Organisational strategy – yes or no?

The obvious initial question to ask is whether your charity has a clear organisational strategy in the first place. If the answer is yes, then congratulations – your task has suddenly become a lot easier. However, this won't always be the case.

Many of the communications heads we consulted told us their organisations either don't have clear strategic objectives or that the objectives are so broad they don't provide an adequate framework for planning.

This is a common problem but it shouldn't stop you in your tracks. If your organisation doesn't have a proper strategy, you could be just the catalyst it needs. Embarking on this process will create dialogue and debate, and may force your colleagues to sharpen up and develop an organisational strategy.

As one of the contributors noted: "Sometimes communications and marketing can hold a big mirror to the organisation and expose gaps and anomalies in the organisational strategy, which isn't always a comfortable process."

Another contributor said: "If the business aims aren't clear, it's important to establish a common interpretation of the organisational plan by talking to others." Likewise, marketing and digital communications consultant Zoe Amar told us: "It's about making sure the business aims are as clear as possible. Sometimes that clarity isn't there and you have to strategise upwards."

Recognising these challenges, you will just have to start your process with a few assumptions and navigate your way from there – strategise upwards, as Zoe puts it. After all, where better to start developing an organisational strategy than a process which asks, "What's our place in the world and our relationship with it?" Those are the questions good communications strategies ask and attempt to answer. So why wait?

> " If I'd had to have all the answers before writing the strategy, it would never have been written. It does as much to acknowledge gaps as it does to propose solutions. A strategy is a point in time. "
>
> **Victoria Shooter, National Deaf Children's Society**

A theory of change

If your organisation has an agreed theory of change, this may provide a useful starting point for your work. A theory of change is a definition of how your organisation believes change happens in terms of the work that it does. Some organisations have written theories of change, others have more of a de facto approach, ie a general agreement on how they do things and what impact that has.

There are a number of established frameworks for theories of change, the most common being a model which describes input, output, outcome, impact and the causal links between them. Search for this online and you will find it easily. One of the best things about having a theory of change is that you don't have to continually remake the case for new projects because you have already agreed on the links between your activity and the benefit you bring to the world.

An example of this might be that your organisation has agreed that if more people know their rights then they will enjoy better lives. If that's the consensus, and the basis of your organisation's business model, you may not have to expend a huge amount of effort proving that your rights awareness campaign is worth doing.

Developing your strategy alongside 'business as usual'

Strategic communications may not comprise all of your work. Normally, part of the function of a communications team is to provide a service to other parts of the organisation – for example, producing materials on request or developing digital content for specific projects. There will also be incidental, unplanned or reactive activity that just needs to get done.

The trick is to be able to identify which is which and invest your team's resources accordingly. Don't try to shoehorn every last activity into your strategy; you can deliver a great service to your colleagues and use brand management to ensure that even those communications projects that fall outside the strategy all hang together.

Starting with a blank sheet

Communicators often get stuck looking at their existing communications and making minor adjustments, feeling burdened by the weight of assumptions about what they are there to do. Sure, you need to start with what you have and build on your success, but sometimes it's more useful to forget about all of that and ask the question: "If I was starting from scratch, what would I do?"

Deciding how communications will support organisational objectives

Try this set of exercises with your team and invite some friendly colleagues from other departments to help you set objectives. There are a few stages, so it's best to split them over a number of sessions to keep the thinking fresh and allow time to pull together notes from each session before moving onto the next stage.

Exercises 4 and 5 should help you think about the strategic purpose of communications for your organisation and step away from 'business as usual'. They are also an opportunity to involve colleagues from other teams and get them on board, since they will have contributed to the thinking. It's also a chance for you and your team to think about where the organisation is going and what colleagues from other departments want from you.

EXERCISE 4:
Listing strategic objectives

- Set the scene by describing in big-picture terms what your organisation does and write up a list of its strategic objectives. This will be the touchstone to check your thinking against throughout the process. Then share insights from your discovery phase. What is your current operating environment and your status within it? What are the strengths and opportunities identified through your research and consultation? These will provide the stimulus to help shape your ideas.

- Now draw a very large Venn diagram, with a circle representing each of the organisation's main external-facing functions. Many non-profits can divide their work into three main areas: service delivery, fundraising and policy/campaigning, so these are used to create the model in our example. You might choose others. This is the framework you will be building from.

- Next, work together to think about all the possible ways communications could deliver for each of those business areas, either in a supporting or lead role. Anything that springs to mind is fine. Capture it all. You can filter later. Eventually these will become your communications functions. Again, generic examples are used here – some will work for you, some won't – so think about the possibilities unique to your organisation.

ORGANISATIONAL FUNCTIONS

SERVICES

Behaviour change

Rights awareness

Service outreach

Community mobilisation

Information & advice

Best practice promotion

Programme documentation

Government influencing

Brand building

Corporate partnerships

POLICY & CAMPAIGNS

FUNDRAISING

Public advocacy

Supporter acquisition & mobilisation

Membership development

Coalition development

Celebrity development

EXERCISE 5:
Deciding what to focus on – affordability vs impact

Having identified all these possibilities, how will you decide what to focus your communications strategy on? Your decisions are likely to be based on a balance of:

Impact Is this activity likely to make a significant contribution to your organisational aims? Would not doing it expose the organisation to unacceptable risk?

Affordability Do you have the resources to deliver this?

Draw a simple graph with two axes titled Impact and Affordability, and invite your colleagues to plot all the possibilities you identified in the previous exercise on this graph.

It should look something like this:

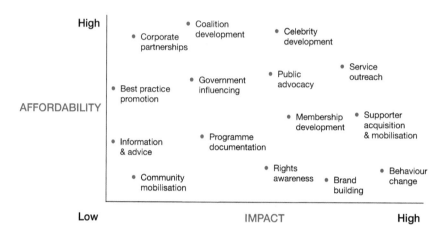

Next, consider what you will focus on. Circle priority areas in one colour (we've used blue) – these are the communications functions that will shape your communications strategy.

Then consider what you will not do (or stop doing) and circle these in another colour (we've used black). This can be difficult but it's likely there are some activities that are making little impact, not cost-efficient, or there is little demand for within the organisation. Your strategy should tell you as much about what you won't do as what you will, otherwise it will lack focus and you could find yourself overstretched.

Anything that's not circled may continue at some level but will not be a top priority in your strategy. Remembering the need to keep some capacity for day-to-day business as usual, you could assign a certain amount of your team capacity, say 20%, to these areas and provide them as a service without creating special project structures to deliver them.

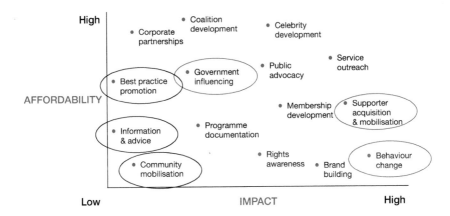

It's important to remember to avoid being enslaved by the process. This exercise is designed to help you solve problems. The chart won't provide all the answers, but it will serve as a useful discussion guide to identify your priority areas. Working through this in a meeting with the right colleagues from across the organisation will help build consensus on your priorities – a vital step you need to go through.

In this example, the chosen activities reflect the need for balance across organisational functions (policy, services and fundraising) and include less 'affordable' areas, recognising that some investment will be needed. There will also be other issues specific to your context that you'll need to think about, such as your board's appetite for investing in brand development or the need to build on existing projects that are already achieving results.

Taking the communications functions you have decided to focus on (in this example we have chosen supporter acquisition, government influencing and behaviour change), you need to start developing objectives. Begin by considering what specific contribution each communications function can make to achieving organisational objectives. Try to use SMART objectives (which are Specific, Measurable, Attainable, Relevant and Time-bound) and introduce key performance indicators (KPIs) that will enable you to measure your success in meeting those objectives. Be bold – you can sense-check the numbers later.

Homes for Youth – aligning organisational and communications objectives

Organisational objective	Increase proportion of voluntary income by 30% over three years to secure sustainable financial future	Young people's access to support services before they become homeless is increased by 20%	Establish affordable housing for young people as a top-five priority at the next election
Communications function	Supporter acquisition	Behaviour change	Government influencing
Communications objective	Increase propensity to support Homes for Youth among target audience	Persuade more young people (14–24) to access services, through rights awareness and service promotion	Strengthen public discourse in the media on affordable housing for young people
Communications KPI	Propensity to support the organisation among target audience increased by 50%	35% of young people (14-24) agree with the statement "I know where to go when facing a housing crisis"	Double broadsheet and broadcast current affairs media visibility of policy on housing for young people

> We created a matrix showing organisational aims, drilled down into communication aims, channels, and so on. This proved to be one of our most useful planning tools.

Mathurot Chuladul, Making Music

Sometimes the direct causal links between your communications and organisational objectives will not be easy to prove. For example, in the Homes for Youth case, more young people knowing where to go in a housing crisis may not be a result of communications activity alone, and may not be the only factor in the increased service uptake. So you will have to make some assumptions at the start on what seems reasonable, and any information on what's worked in the past will help. As Ben Hewitt from Save the Children International said, "You have to build consensus around a theory of change, of how to attribute outcomes to your work, because sometimes it takes a leap of faith."

With this table, we have the basis of your strategy, which you can continue to build on, adding brand goals, audiences, messaging, and so on.

We have to demonstrate that all our activity is contributing to the target of reducing asthma attacks by 50% in the next five years. This clarity is very helpful.

Claudine Snape, Asthma UK

Crisis communications – be prepared

One area of communications that may be set apart from your organisational objectives is crisis communications. Nevertheless, you will need to ensure you have assigned adequate capacity to it.

Bad news travels fast, and these days it can travel even faster. Whether they are true or not, damaging stories about your organisation can reach thousands of people in a matter of minutes. Similarly, if a crisis prevents you doing your work and delivering services, it can permanently damage your reputation and even put you out of business. If crisis strikes, you need to make sure you have the right procedures and resources in place, and that staff are aware of them. You are going to need:

- A crisis communications team in place, including a crisis management lead person and spokesperson.

- A rapid assessment of the situation and what's likely to happen next, who will be affected, what the organisation needs to do (immediately and in the longer term) and who needs to do it.

- Key messages for key audiences – media, supporters, beneficiaries, staff and partners.

By mapping out a clear, workable crisis communications plan (and revising it often) you can emerge from a potential disaster with your image intact – maybe even enhanced.

CASE STUDY: **CLIC Sargent: Set a strategic direction**

Lorraine Clifton, CEO, and Liz North, director of communications and campaigning, CLIC Sargent

CLIC Sargent's strategic direction defines our course for 2011–16 and highlights our ambition to ensure that all children and young people up to the age of 25 who have been diagnosed with cancer can access a range of services that meet their needs.

After a review of our vision and purpose, we reaffirmed our vision as 'A world where children and young people with cancer live life to the full', clarifying that we meant both during treatment and for the rest of their lives. We then focused on defining the most important forms of support we could offer, considering both the areas of greatest need and where CLIC Sargent was providing support that wasn't available elsewhere. We defined our purpose as being to:

- Reduce the practical and financial impact of treatment on a child or young person and their family
- Support the emotional wellbeing and resilience of children, young people and their families
- Maximise the time that children and young people can spend safely at home during treatment
- Maximise children and young people's potential by giving them access to education, training and employment.

This purpose now drives all our decisions on what we do and (often harder) on what we leave to others. The next step was to set the organisational objectives that would deliver these long-range outcomes over the period of the strategy. These are:

- Understand and meet the needs of children and young people and their families
- Deliver improved outcomes for children and young people with cancer and their families through evidence-based clinical, social, emotional and practical support (including bereavement support)
- Influence decision-makers at all levels, from the school head to Secretary of State, so that children and young people can live life to the full
- Increase voluntary income to reach more children and young people with cancer and stay financially resilient
- Keep building an effective, efficient organisation and work with partners and supporters for greater impact.

The development of these objectives was based on analysis and learnings from the more detailed functional strategies then being developed which would underpin our strategic direction.

Trustees, who sign off on all the main functional strategies, were closely involved in the development of the strategic direction. Directors presented functional strategy development frameworks to trustees at dedicated workshops, which encouraged challenge and debate.

Once our strategic direction and services strategy were completed, we then developed our influencing, fundraising and financial strategies, and are currently at the concluding stages of developing a digital strategy.

The communications department at CLIC Sargent includes policy and influencing and the information service, so the director of communications and campaigning was at the heart of strategic discussions from the start, and 'owned' the Influencing strategy (which included corporate communications elements).

As a busy charity with limited capacity, we must develop our strategy alongside business as usual, and ensure key staff have time, space and support to contribute to strategy development. We are only now starting to develop our communications strategy, which will sit alongside the functional strategies and help deliver corporate objectives.

This means we can craft a communications strategy that is specifically linked to our organisational and functional strategic objectives, as well as enabling effective awareness-raising of our cause and impact.

A separate communications strategy will mean we can look across the functional and corporate strategies and pull out communications elements, including stakeholder audiences, channels and messages. We'll use this data to inform the strategy and define and identify communications priorities for the organisation. This will help us set out a vision for communications that will hopefully enable the whole organisation to see the benefits to them, and their work, of a strategic approach to communications.

Achieving integration through shared objectives

Many communications directors say that the Holy Grail of communications is integration. This can mean any number of things, from loose alignment of messages to tightly managed communication programmes designed to achieve multiple objectives.

Generally speaking, integration means developing audience-centred communications approaches that overcome internal divisions and deliver a range of aims simultaneously. This might include fundraising, campaigning, service outreach or brand building.

It's no surprise that communications teams are such strong advocates of integration. They are likely to see most of the organisation's communications outputs and the many conflicting and muddled messages received by their audiences. They are in a unique position where they can spot both the missed opportunities resulting from isolated activities and the potential for more joined-up working that's present in every organisation.

The place of communications in an organisation's structure

Achieving integration is one of the many strong arguments for communications being a stand-alone department, headed by someone who sits on the senior management team. This gives them a broad view and the independence to act as advocates for their audiences. It allows them to directly serve the organisational strategy, as opposed to being an instrument of fundraising or policy with a narrower view of their role. An alternative approach that some organisations take is for all the major communicating functions (eg fundraising, communications and campaigns) to be brought together into a single division, while making room for a strong, distinctive role and voice for each function, with executive-level representation for all. This can work better for smaller organisations that have to take extra care to avoid top-heavy management structures.

The place of communications within an organisation's structure divides opinion and is often a topic of fierce debate. However, the key to delivering integrated communications isn't just about structure, but is about cross-departmental working and promoting a culture of collaboration.

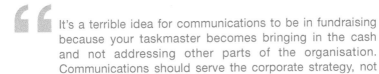

> It's a terrible idea for communications to be in fundraising because your taskmaster becomes bringing in the cash and not addressing other parts of the organisation. Communications should serve the corporate strategy, not the fundraising strategy.
>
> **Richard Davidson, Anthony Nolan**

> At Friends of the Earth, the Fundraising, Communications and Activism department has an emphasis on thinking strategically about engagement as a more joined-up package. People don't divide their support into time, money or voice, so why should we?
>
> **Adeela Warley, Friends of the Earth**

The most frequently cited driver for integrated strategies is when different departments within organisations are reaching similar audiences, whether through design or coincidence. This is to be expected because any given person may come into contact with your organisation in any number of different capacities. For example, in her or his professional role, someone may be a potential corporate donor, a target of your policy influencing, or even a prospective employee of your organisation, while in their private life they may be a donor, service user or activist. Effective integration means that when that person comes into contact with your organisation through different channels – whether it be email, direct mail or a news report – they have a positive experience that strengthens their engagement since those different modes of communication reinforce each other.

This doesn't mean that every piece of communication you produce should be intended to achieve multiple aims. Some might, but often that won't be appropriate. But it does mean that all of your material should be part of a coherent story and that you have taken the time internally to plan your communications output from an audience perspective.

Benefits of integration

From conversations with contributors to this book, we found the three most commonly cited benefits of integration are:

- **Deeper engagement of audiences through richer and more diverse content**

  Given that your audiences wear many hats, it's likely they will be happy to engage with your organisation in different ways. For example, some fundraisers find that their supporters like engaging in political campaign actions, because it strengthens their commitment to the cause which in turn reduces donor attrition rates. Similarly in some sectors, particularly health-related charities, many service users go on to become donors or advocates, and so they appreciate exposure to the different modes of engagement your organisation offers.

- **Greater coherence of message and brand**

  If your audiences are getting conflicting messages from your organisation, you will ultimately fail to communicate anything with clarity and impact, not to mention the risk to reputation. Greater coherence will make your messages work harder, achieve more cut-through and result in bigger impact.

- **More efficient use of resources**

  Taking an holistic view of your communications output will inevitably expose overlapping activities that can be easily merged or opportunities to share resources and improve quality. A good example of this is commissioned content, such as case studies of beneficiaries or service users. These can be repurposed in lots of different contexts if they are commissioned wisely.

Planning together

This triple whammy of deeper engagement, greater coherence and improved efficiency should be good enough reasons to strive for a more integrated approach. But unless you address integration at the outset and link it to your annual planning and budgeting round, it may only achieve superficial, ad hoc benefits. Working together with other teams at the strategic planning stage – sharing objectives and recognising you need each other's help to succeed – will help you achieve a win-win.

It's important to recognise at the outset that different departments and functions are motivated by different things, and may describe 'success' in quite different terms than you would. Fundraisers, unsurprisingly, are primarily focused on raising money, and will be preoccupied with improving return on investment through, for example, driving down their cost per acquisition or improving supporter retention. Your policy team, on the other hand, want their knockout research and arguments delivered to opinion leaders and the decision-makers they influence. Neither are likely to compromise their aims in order to engage in your vision to be the best-loved brand in your sector, and so may consider integrated working to be a bureaucratic headache. So you will have to show them that working together – and with you – will give them success on their terms. They won't do it for you; they will do it if they see how it benefits them and helps them meet their own objectives.

So how will integrating a project with you help fundraisers raise more funds? And how will it help lobbyists achieve more influence? You will need to find the answers to questions such as this. Here are some examples of mutually beneficial integration:

- **Popular mobilisation campaigns** (eg letter writing or petitioning) that improve brand preference for your organisation may result in lower cost per acquisition for new donors or a 'warm' prospect pool for conversion. This achieves outcomes for both campaigns and fundraising teams, so can you plan campaigns together to ensure you maximise this opportunity?

- **Targeted campaigns** that improve rights awareness and service uptake will build your reputation and directly achieve charitable aims, as well as affect the demographic and number of beneficiaries. This may then enhance your capacity to influence policy at local authority level, which could achieve outcomes for services and policy teams, so working together on how you would target such a project could achieve a win for everyone.

- **Media activity** on public policy issues will have implications for your direct lobbying work. It may, for example, result in more requests for comment through the media and invitations to participate in policy forums, but it may also position your organisation in such a way as to improve statutory funding. This achieves outcomes for policy and fundraising teams, so could you align this activity at the annual planning stage?

> An example of an integrated campaign was our 'Look, Smile, Chat' campaign, which aimed to encourage kids to communicate with deaf children in their schools. We engaged multiple teams and departments in the organisation, and there was a single integrated plan for everyone. All of the briefing was done by a single project manager.
>
> Objectives across the teams included fundraising (linked to a community fundraising initiative), new members (through a free membership scheme), and profile for the issue and the brand. We learned about the need for internal staff in other teams to use common planning tools – prior to this, people had worked in a quite unstructured way. It's a constant battle to get people to understand what communications can achieve so it was a good start from a relatively low base.

Victoria Shooter, National Deaf Children's Society

When you start to develop your communications strategy, try to work with other teams to develop shared objectives that are reflected in their plans and meet their own objectives. Many of the directors we consulted said that having similar or related KPIs across departments helped achieve integration for them, and integrated working, project by project, has flowed naturally from that.

EXERCISE 6:
Integrated objectives and KPIs

If you do persuade colleagues to participate in developing a more integrated strategy, try building on the log frame we developed earlier, and working with your colleagues to add their objectives and KPIs. This can be a useful way of showing the inter-dependence between your different functions, and will give you a framework for ongoing planning. In our example, based on the Homes for Youth charity, we have focused on the fundraising, policy and campaigns, and services teams' departmental objectives and KPIs.

Department objectives and KPIs	Organisational objective	Increase proportion of voluntary income by 30% over three years to secure sustainable financial future	Young people's access to support services before they become homeless is increased by 20%	Establish affordable housing for young people as a top-five priority at the next election
	Communications function	Supporter acquisition	Behaviour change	Government influencing
	Communications objective	Increase propensity to support Homes for Youth among target audience	Persuade more young people (14–24) to access services, through rights awareness and service promotion	Strengthen public discourse in the media on affordable housing for young people
	Communications KPI	Propensity to support the organisation among target audience increased by 50%	35% of young people (14-24) agree with the statement "I know where to go when facing a housing crisis"	Double broadsheet and broadcast current affairs media visibility of policy on housing for young people
	Fundraising objective	Increase voluntary income through optimising individual giving programme	Mobilise funding partners to promote services through their media channels	Cross sell campaign petitions to donor network, to demonstrate popular support for the issue
	Fundraising KPI	Recruit and maintain 10,000 regular givers, with cost per acquisition reduced by 15%	Three major funding partners agree to support rights awareness campaign and deliver significant exposure	At least 10% donors take a campaign action
	Policy & campaigns objective	Cross-sell fundraising 'asks' to campaigner network	Policy makers incorporate rights awareness programmes into services for young people	Increase political support for better housing for vulnerable young people in three main political parties
	Policy & campaigns KPI	At least 10% campaigners make a donation	50% new statutory programmes for young people include a rights awareness programme	Double importance of housing for young people in parliamentary monitoring, and the issue appears in three main political parties' manifestos
	Services objective	Identify projects in need of increased voluntary funding, and provide supporter-friendly impact monitoring	Enhance capacity for service delivery both directly and through partnerships	Use local authority relationships to demonstrate positive impact of low-cost housing schemes for young people and build political momentum at constituency level
	Services KPI	£2m of fundable projects identified, and annual impact reporting delivered	Increase capacity of face to face services by 20%	50% local projects hold meetings with local authority housing leads on topic

When not to integrate

Sometimes the resistance you experience is reasonable. There will be situations where integrated planning requires a lot of effort that isn't justified by results, especially when targeting a very niche audience or on very small, ad hoc projects.

Similarly, there are situations where an integrated approach can be counter-productive. For example, one person we spoke to told us they take great care to create distance between their national campaigns and their local services in order to balance their critic/friend relationship with local authorities.

You will need to consider what, for your organisation, the benefits of integration are and when it's better to work independently. However, if you choose to integrate, you will need to ensure you are working with a strong evidence base, both to make the case for integration and to figure out whether it's delivering the benefits you predicted. Tracking your shared KPIs will help you do this.

CASE STUDY: Integration starts with strategy

John Grounds, deputy chief executive, RSPCA

As part of our organisational strategic review, we're looking at current perceptions of the RSPCA. Our research shows that at the top level, the charity is very well known, trusted, respected and admired. At the next level, however, there is no consistency of view about things we do other than our work with companion animals such as cats and dogs. In fact, we also work with research animals, farm animals and wildlife, and not only in the UK.

We need to move people on and attract new supporters who need to know about our other work. We've experimented with a more integrated approach on a small scale, with our emergency appeal before Christmas 2012. This campaign aimed to raise awareness of an impending animal welfare crisis in the UK and ask for funds to help us meet the increasing need. At a simple level, this integrated several strands: a fundraising ask, digital activity and PR. As a result, we got strong message delivery and enhanced return on investment with the fundraising element. We've used this as a simple model to show how everyone benefits in terms of team objectives.

We followed the Christmas appeal with our RSPCA Week for 2013: 'Time to care, time to act'. It was the most integrated campaign in the history of the RSPCA Week. Traditionally, it has been about local branches collecting money outside local supermarkets – itself a very valuable activity, but not the full picture. This year we focused much more on celebrating what the RSPCA is about. We launched our annual Prosecutions Report (known as the 'cruelty stats') during RSPCA Week, whereas previously we'd have brought it out at a different time. We ran a range of linked fundraising activities – including direct mail activity – before, during and after the week, as well as digital projects and lots of internal staff activities. We ran a linked campaign action on tougher sentencing for animal abusers during the week too.

Planning is now carried out collectively across the directorate, with the new organisational strategy providing the context. Individual teams will still have individual targets – fundraising, for example, will have targets relating to different income streams, but within an overall integrated strategy. It's about maximising opportunities. The teams have shared key performance indicators around RSPCA Week and the Christmas emergency appeal, and the new strategy will set shared KPIs across all our activity.

We're beginning to build our understanding of our audiences and the touch points they have with us, but we have more work to do on this. We're in the early stages but are already working on treating campaigners as potential donors and vice versa, not just as distinct groups.

Integration at a brand and strategy level is key, but that doesn't mean every single piece of communications is identical at all times. Sometimes there will be absolute integration of messages for a particular campaign, while at other times there could be specific messages to specific audiences within an overarching integrated brand approach.

One of the key benefits of integration has been the reinforcement of our brand and core message, and a real clarity as to what is and is not appropriate for us to be doing.

Action points from Chapter 3

- Start from a blank sheet and explore how communications can support organisational objectives.

- Involve colleagues in the process.

- Be bold in your prioritisation – you can't do it all, so decide what you will focus on for greatest impact.

- Look for opportunities for more integrated working and develop shared objectives and key performance indicators (KPIs) with other departments.

- Again, don't be enslaved by the process. It's designed to help you and your colleagues think creatively.

4

Knowing your audiences

Imagine trying to hold a conversation with someone who's standing on the other side of a closed door. You can't see them or hear them and you don't know anything about them. In fact, you are not even sure if they are there at all. What will you talk about?

The fact is that unless you know who you are talking to, communication is pointless, so it's impossible to develop a credible communications strategy unless you know who your audiences are. And it follows that the better you know your audiences, the more effective your communications will be. This may seem obvious, but surprisingly it's often overlooked.

Many organisations will struggle to tell you who their audiences are, with some only having a vague notion of who they are trying to reach. Some use terms such as 'general public' which, when you think about it, simply means 'everyone' or 'everyone else'. Others define their audiences according to the channel they reach them through – for example, 'web users' – or by their value to the organisation ('regular givers' or 'campaigners'). None of these definitions tell organisations anything useful about who their audiences are, what they think or what will motivate them to engage. Audience free strategies are like dropping stones into a deep dark well – so deep you can't hear the splash. Down goes the annual report, the email bulletins, the press releases – and standing at the top of the well, a communications manager saying, "OK, but at least I'm communicating, right?" Wrong.

Some organisations define their audiences too narrowly, constraining their thinking to people they are already talking to – their donors, parliamentary contacts or existing service users, for example – and forget to think about the new, bigger audiences they could reach, audiences which could help the organisation grow or extend its circle of influence. This is a limiting perspective because, for organisations to survive, they need to be constantly thinking about the new conversations they can start with people they don't yet know.

At the centre of every good communications strategy is a clear definition of its audiences.

Defining your audiences

As you develop your strategy, you should make time for this. You will need to consider the demographics (including age, sex, ethnicity, education, income and location) of your audiences and their attitudes to the issues you communicate about and the people you help. You will need to know what you want your audiences to think, feel and do, and what will motivate them to engage with you. And critically, you will need to know as much as possible about how they use media – which websites they visit, which newspapers they read and how active they are in social media.

Audience size is also important. You need to define a big enough audience so you can make a reasonable impact, yet small enough to reach with enough frequency to get noticed. For example, in the case of mass public audiences for brand building and fundraising, even the largest UK charities might define an audience of only a few million people (from the UK's population of about 60 million) they want to reach, say, 10 times a year, while recognising that many more people will be exposed to their communications much less frequently.

Defining mass-market audiences

There are numerous tools you can use to define mass-market audiences. Probably the three best-known are TGI (Target Group Index, run by Kantar Media), MOSAIC (from Experian) and ACORN (from CACI). The tools are similar to one another in that they define audience segments on the basis of large, ongoing consumer surveys, and offer quite sophisticated modelling tools. Some, like ACORN, offer pre-defined audience segments (or typologies) such as Educated Urbanites or

Affluent Greys, while others (for example, TGI) provide tools for defining your own audiences, which can be used to drill down to small segments in a lot of depth. Using a combination of these tools you could, for example, identify an audience group that:

- Is likely to donate to social welfare charities
- Is interested in current affairs
- Often changes its voting patterns
- Is a word-of-mouth influencer among their friends.

Once you have selected your audience, these tools will tell you about their attitude and behaviour trends in relation to a range of other subjects and, vitally, about their media consumption.

Few charities keep their own subscriptions to these audience segmentation tools. Usually they commission communications agencies to help with this. If you have an external marketing or media planning agency, consider asking them to support you in developing your audience segmentations. If this is not an option, you could consider free sources of information since many media companies, such as TV channels, newspapers and magazines, share information about their audiences. You can also access demographic information free from the Office for National Statistics, and some polling companies offer limited data for free. With a bit of creativity and head-scratching, you may be able to piece together data from various sources and come up with some useable audience definitions – depending on what information is available about your field of work.

Who's your bull's-eye?

In the course of your three-year strategy period, it's likely you will reach a lot of people at some point or another. Depending on your approach, this could amount to millions, even in the case of the smallest charities.

An important principle in really effective mass communications is knowing how to balance reach with frequency. That's the number of people you communicate to (reach) and the amount of times you communicate with them (frequency). So while 10 million people may come across you once or twice over the course of a year, who are the 250,000 that will encounter you 10 times in the same period? This is your bull's-eye.

Your bull's-eye target audience comprises the people you will reach more often than anyone else, enough to see a change in their awareness and understanding of your organisation. It should be a fairly small number of people – probably less than one million for all but the largest charities. Consider targeting people most likely to be 'word-of-mouth influencers'. They will help spread the word and act as your ambassadors in their own communities without you even knowing about it.

Your bull's-eye audience should not be the sole focus of your public communications, but as you plan individual communications initiatives, you should try to include them every time you communicate. Over time, these people will become the audience you keep going back to, who will start to see the world as a place filled with your message and your issues.

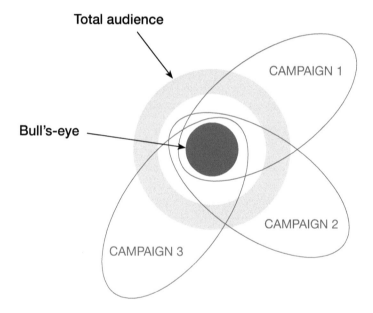

This diagram shows how a bull's-eye audience is not the only group you reach, but is the one you reach every time.

Other audiences

Of course, some of your audiences will not be defined by segmenting the general public because they will be more niche or specialist, in which case planning tools based on national statistics may be of limited use. For example, you may want to reach people with a specific health condition or opinion leaders in a specific policy area. In defining these audiences, you will need to figure out the best way to reach and research them, and your approach will be different in almost every case. Some audience groups can be found through membership associations or specialist websites, publications and social networks, and it should be possible to use these routes to explore and define your niche audiences.

Shared audiences

If you can, it's a good idea to work with other departments to get a shared understanding of who your audiences are and look for overlaps. For example, you may find an audience group that's likely to both donate money and support your campaigns or a segment among your service users who may be predisposed to donating. So working across functions on an audience segmentation that delivers for both your fundraising and campaigning teams could help you achieve the more integrated approach we looked at in the previous chapter.

Furthermore, some of the more sophisticated audience strategies move away from the idea that different departments 'own' different audiences, and that any given audience serves only one function for the organisation. Instead they recognise the overlaps, developing integrated plans centred on audiences and agreeing protocols for who can communicate with whom and when.

Talking to people about 'their' audiences was a huge challenge. Teams perceived 'their' audiences as being different and therefore not to be included in the audience audit. From politicians to local authority commissioners, we heard over and over that teams knew how to communicate with these special people. Unlocking access to these audiences took a lot of cajoling and promises that we weren't going to ride roughshod over years of relationship building. One of the keys to overcoming this tension was talking about stewardship as opposed to management as somehow it sounds less controlling.

Emma Harrison, ex-Mencap

New and existing audiences

To help you achieve growth in impact, influence or income, you may need to reach some new audiences. In this case you'll need to differentiate between them and your existing audiences – ie the people you are already talking to. Sometimes your growth plans will be 'more of the same', suggesting that new audiences will be similar to existing audiences, so learning about who you are already engaging is a good place to start. Alternatively, you may want to reach into entirely new areas, in which case you are starting with a blank page. A common example of this is using engagement campaigns to reach an audience slightly younger than your existing donor base, with the expectation that they will move on to supporting you through donations to keep your finances looking healthy. In any case, your strategy should be clear about the distinction between existing and new audiences to avoid confusion.

Reaching your audiences

Whatever tools and techniques you use to define your audiences, make sure they tell you as much as possible about your audiences' media consumption. Avoid making the common mistake of defining audiences without considering how to reach them, otherwise your segmentation work risks being an intellectual exercise with little practical use.

Using research to understand your audiences

Once you have decided who your target audiences are, the next step is to get to know them better through research. This will help you understand more about how they feel and think about your issues and your brand, and what will motivate them to engage. Research helps keep you audience-centred and ensures that whatever communication work you do, it's developed specifically with them in mind.

Research also helps challenge your own thinking about what your audiences want, since we often work with the default – and often false – assumption that the people we're communicating with have similar opinions, interests and motivations to our own. This is a common mistake – for example campaigners often target people just like themselves, when in some cases they may achieve more political impact by mobilising middle-England swing voters who wouldn't be seen dead at a Hyde Park rally.

Audience research is used to:

- **Consult people who know your organisation**

  Asking your supporters or members what they would like you to work on, for example, or what information they would like from you can be very enlightening.

- **Inform your thinking**

  Early in your strategy development, you may benefit from some fresh perspectives around your audiences' attitudes to your organisation or issues.

- **Evolve an idea**

  It's sometimes useful to get feedback from your audiences during the development of a new communications initiative to help shape your work. What do you like about this campaign? What would prompt you to engage? What would put you off?

- **Test your work**

  When your ideas are more fully formed, you can use quantitative testing to provide hard data about whether it's likely to work. This is particularly relevant for digital communications and traditional marketing channels, where you have control over your output and targeting. It's less so in PR and news media.

Audience research can also provide you with evidence to inform your decisions (around how to position a policy issue or which channels to invest in, for example) and can help build consensus among colleagues around your decisions. It's quite common to find old and untested assumptions about what audiences want being used to argue against change. In these situations, a little audience research can be the very thing to break internal deadlocks and move organisations forward.

Research helps remind us that we are not our own audience and that the people we're communicating with may have a different point of view from our own.

Athena Lamnisos, Community Links

It's always useful

There's a tendency to only conduct audience research in the context of marketing communications activity with bigger budgets attached, which usually means fundraising or brand building. But audience research is just as important when developing strategies with smaller budgets, which are likely to rely on news media, PR, digital and other relatively low-cost channels. In all cases, the principle remains the same: the better you know your audience, the more effective your communications will be.

It doesn't have to be expensive...

Many of the people we spoke to for this book talked about audience research as a luxury for those with big budgets. But with the rise of digital technologies, some forms of audience research have become much cheaper. It's now possible to poll large numbers of people very quickly or conduct more qualitative research online. For example, you can use your own online communities, such as Facebook supporters, or engage in other internet discussions. You could even try the old-fashioned way and telephone 20 of your supporters, partners, beneficiaries or campaign targets to ask for their views. Most people love to be asked their opinion and you will probably find they are very happy to talk.

There are also an increasing number of free online tools for canvasing ideas and opinion. Search 'free crowdsourcing tools' and you will find plenty.

...but outsource if you can

Having said that, if budgets allow, it's a good idea to commission research externally. Involving specialist, independent researchers is likely to lead to more credible results that your colleagues will trust. External people will also bring a completely fresh perspective, untainted by preconceptions. Whatever method you use, don't skip audience research.

What do you want to find out?

Before you start designing your research programme, you need to decide what you want to know. The more specific your question, the more useable the findings will be. The worst question you can ask is, "What do people think about us?" since it will certainly give you vague or irrelevant results. More useful questions might be, "What does this audience like and dislike about this campaign idea?" or "What brand attributes will make this audience more likely to donate to us?" or "How would this audience like to receive health information?".

Whatever questions you ask and whatever research methods you use, the findings won't make your decisions for you. They are there to provide data and ideas to help inform your decisions. It's important to see research as a starting point, not an end goal. So think first about what decisions are going to be informed by the research findings and make sure the people around you understand this when creating the questions and deciding on which research methods to use.

> Research is about solving a specific business problem so you should start with a clear understanding of what you want to do with the research.

Zoe Amar

> When going into research, it's important to know what question you are trying to answer. That may not be as simple as a single sentence. If it's about a particular group, you need to break it down and be clear who you are talking to. You also need to make sure you don't steer the conversation too much. A decent research company will advise you on how to avoid bias.

Richard Davidson, Anthony Nolan

CASE STUDY: Lullaby Trust: Ask the audience

Emma Taggart, Lullaby Trust

The Lullaby Trust, which changed its name from FSID (Foundation for the Study of Infant Deaths) in April 2013, provides expert advice on safer sleep for babies, supports bereaved families and raises awareness of sudden infant death.

After more than 40 years as FSID, changing the charity's name was a big decision. The chief executive, some trustees and most staff were utterly convinced of the need for change but others, including some bereaved parents with a long-standing connection and attachment to FSID, were more cautious about making a break with the past.

The charity commissioned research in two phases to help it understand why it needed to change its name and how it could better connect with its target audiences, particularly young parents living in difficult circumstances who are most at risk of experiencing the sudden and unexpected death of a baby.

Qualitative research in the form of interviews and focus groups with selected stakeholders was conducted to discover how FSID was perceived by its key audiences, including young parents. The research revealed that the name FSID was considered old-fashioned, cold and scary. It was failing to connect with the very people who most needed to hear the charity's safer sleep messages.

This initial research enabled trustees to view the charity through the eyes of young parents and others with whom the charity needed to communicate more effectively. The results were instrumental in persuading trustees that the name had to change if the charity was to succeed in its ambition to halve the number of babies dying suddenly and without identifiable cause by 2020.

Once the decision to change was made, the initial research findings helped staff and expert branding consultants to develop several potential new names for the charity. Two of these potential names were put out to public consultation in the second phase of market research.

Further interviews and focus groups were undertaken with the original group of stakeholders to explore reactions to the new names (and accompanying visual identity options). A quantitative survey enabled the charity to test potential names with a larger sample of people. A simple online survey was publicised on various online forums and the charity made good use of its existing social media channels by posting the survey on its Facebook page and Twitter feed. It also built relationships with like-minded charities and organisations willing to support its research activity. Netmums and Bounty both promoted the survey to their own social networks to drive additional traffic to the online survey. Around 1,000 people responded to the survey over eight days.

The results of the survey showed a clear preference for one name. The nuanced feedback from interviews and focus groups provided additional context as to why people preferred one name and visual identity rather than another.

Although the findings were only one factor influencing the final decision, the research was crucial to persuading trustees and staff to adopt its new name. Without the evidence provided by the research, it would have been harder for the charity to embrace change. The research findings also proved useful when explaining the name change to long-standing supporters, including bereaved parents, some of whom were unsure at first that changing the name was the right thing to do but have been reassured by the market research.

The charity was clear from the start that the research was intended to guide decision-making rather than to provide definitive answers. Although it would be unwise to make a decision in complete contradiction of market research findings, staff and trustees exercised their own judgement rather than relying on the research to make their decisions for them. The research evidence acted as a sense check and provided important guidance.

The key challenge throughout was how to conduct robust market research quickly and cheaply. The charity had a tiny budget for this work and was very fortunate to secure pro bono support from an agency, whose head of insight worked tirelessly to devise, run and interpret the online survey in a matter of days. Qualitative research was carried out by specialist brand consultants who were able to elicit rich feedback from a range of stakeholders despite our constrained budget.

The key lesson from The Lullaby Trust's experience is that one does not have to spend a lot of money on market research to gain useful feedback. Although the charity recognises its research spend was limited, it feels that the results reinforced professional advice received from brand consultants and gave reassurance to trustees that they were making the right decision.

What kind of research?

There are many different research methods and different ways research can be used. It's important to have a clear approach from the outset or you risk tying yourself in knots.

Methods include polls and surveys, focus groups, one-to-one interviews, diary-keeping, and more in-depth 'ethnographic' research where audiences' behaviours are observed by researchers who follow them around with notepads.

Quantitative or qualitative?

Some research methods will give you 'quantitative' data, which comes from polls and surveys that put questions to a large group of people. With quantitative research, usually the aim is to test a large enough sample of the population to be able to extrapolate the results into more generalised findings. For example, a well-designed quantitative study of 2,000 people may be reliable enough to tell you that about 14% of the UK population has heard of your organisation or that 53% of the public believe that bad housing is the greatest challenge faced by young people – both with a fairly small margin of error.

This kind of insight into attitudes of the overall population can be useful for getting a general picture. However, it's likely you will find it far more useful to understand what your target audiences think. For example, if you are an international development NGO, you might want to know more about the views of people who have donated to your sector over the past 12 months, which at the moment stands at around five million people in the UK. In this case, you would need a much larger survey sample of perhaps five or 10 thousand people so that you can focus on the sub-set of people you are interested in, without a huge margin of error in the data.

Other methods provide 'qualitative' insight. These include focus groups and interviews where smaller numbers of people are involved and more nuanced findings are gathered. For example, a focus group may tell you that some people find your campaign idea 'too negative' or it may uncover associations you hadn't thought of: for example that your upbeat PR work on homelessness issues in lifestyle magazines makes you come across as a bit glib.

It's important to understand the difference between quantitative and qualitative research, because they are used differently. Quantitative research is employed to create statistical data, while qualitative research provides more in-depth knowledge that can inform your thinking and help you develop ideas. However, qualitative research cannot be extrapolated to a bigger population without further quantitative testing.

It's generally unwise to use results from qualitative research as a definitive basis for decision-making. In the 'too negative' example above, your focus group may have preferred positive campaigns as they didn't want to think about an uncomfortable subject and have talked each other into a shared point of view. So it would be unwise to immediately stop the campaign. Still, the research is useful because it allows you to reflect that an unknown number of people may consider the campaign too negative. You could then take further action such as quantitative testing, comparing it to a more positive message.

Combining quantitative with qualitative

Qualitative and quantitative research are often used together. Typically, a series of focus groups or interviews are used to identify issues that are then further explored and tested through quantitative methods. This approach helps strengthen objectivity in research, avoiding the risk that if you design your quantitative research on your own, you may bias the survey and end up simply reaffirming things you already know.

 CASE STUDY: Médecins Sans Frontières: Gaining insights into attitudes

Polly Markandya, head of communications, Médecins Sans Frontières

In 2008 I conducted an in-depth study of the UK's public perception and awareness of Médecins Sans Frontières. We'd been in the UK for about 15 years at that time but had never done a proper survey before. The first thing we did was organise, with the help of our advertising agency, a handful of focus groups around the country – in London, York and Exeter. These helped us devise questions to explore further in the other studies. There were, of course, things we knew we wanted to explore, but the focus groups also threw up issues that had never occurred to us. We then ran an omnibus survey to give us some statistically valid data, but this is an expensive thing to do and so we were limited in what we could ask. Finally, and perhaps most usefully, we went around the country ourselves with clipboards and stopped around 1,400 people in parks, railways stations and at bus stops to see what they knew and thought.

The 'vox pop' street survey we carried out ourselves was statistically unsound in that we were not able to ensure that we were fairly assessing all socio-economic and demographic groups. We were limited in the number of personal questions we felt we could ask of street respondents and sometimes had to make guesses about their age or socio-economic status. Nevertheless, the fact that the percentage of people that were aware of us in our vox-pop and omnibus surveys were very similar gave us some confidence in the results we got.

In the vox-pop interviews, we were able to gain a richer insight into people's attitudes to MSF than we might ever have been able to achieve otherwise. Shortly afterwards, I became the head of communications and I feel that involving staff from around the office with interviewing the public helped with buy-in and support to the communications strategies we developed as a result. It helped pop the narrow humanitarian bubble that many of us live in and helped them see the necessity in investing in certain areas of communications and fundraising.

Some things to watch out for

What we say is not always what we do

It's important to recognise that reported behaviour is often different from actual behaviour. A common example is that when UK adults are polled about their likelihood to donate to a specific fundraising campaign, many more say they will support it than actually do once the campaign is rolled out. You will see similar effects in focus groups. This is not due to lack of benevolence on their part – far from it. It's likely a result of a range of barriers, including busy lifestyles, insufficient exposure to the campaign or how easy it is to donate. This also happens because some people respond to research by presenting an idealised version of themselves, offering answers they would like to be true. And who wouldn't like to think of themselves as generous and charitable?

Don't expect your audiences to make sense...

Another thing to watch out for is that research often comes up with seemingly irrational responses or irreconcilable contradictions. A common example is where audiences simultaneously complain that a) your charity spends too much on communications, and b) they never hear enough about you.

Another interesting contradiction is that currently in the UK there are more people who believe we should give international aid than there are people who believe international aid is effective in reducing poverty. This can only mean there is a large section of the UK population that supports international aid but doesn't believe it works. Bad research? No, this is validated by numerous different studies. In fact, once you understand what's behind this, the contradiction begins to make sense. It turns out that many people believe we should give aid as a moral imperative, and this imperative is bigger than their own concerns about aid effectiveness. That's one of the key insights informing campaigning on international aid today: we believe it's the right thing to do and should work hard to make it as effective as possible – a perfectly reasonable and commonly held point of view.

...and you don't have to agree with them

It's also worth noting that people participating in research often resist unfamiliar ideas, preferring familiar, unchallenging options. It's important to be mindful of this because if you are working for a non-profit organisation, it's likely that you are trying to effect change, which can involve communicating new and difficult issues. A case in point: a few years ago I changed the logo of a big UK charity – a household name – and took the new options to a focus group. We had to be honest with ourselves, the focus group didn't like our work much, finding it a bit 'weird' and not really 'like a charity'. But when we turned the conversation to questions like 'what kind of charity would have a logo like this?' they gave answers that worked well for us ('challenging', 'passionate' etc.), and this gave us the confidence to press ahead with our ideas, and helped us create really strong key messages. Fortunately it worked – and two years later our brand 'preference' indicators had almost doubled. Now – think of all the things that have happened in the charity sector that may never have got past a focus group. Important things like issues and campaigns (not just logos) that would not have seen the light of day. Disability rights? Renewable energy?

The key lesson here is use focus groups to explore ideas. Don't ask them to tell you what to do.

Achieving consensus around results

It's important to get agreement between relevant departments about what your research is telling you. Any research can throw up a range of interpretations, both in terms of the actual results and how the organisation should respond. If this isn't managed carefully, your research could prove counter-productive by entrenching different points of view rather than driving consensus.

EXERCISE 7:
Getting to know your audiences through persona development

One way to understand your audiences is to create personas representing each one you want to reach. Begin with what you learned through your research about your beneficiaries, your supporters or your campaign targets. Use your demographic and attitude information then work with colleagues to develop a persona – or a written 'pen portrait' – of each audience type. Don't make general statements about a type of person; instead, have in mind a specific person, defining how old they are, how they spend their time and with whom, what they spend their money on, what they care about, and so on. You are being creative here, but you are not making this up. The personas you develop should be based on your knowledge of who you want to communicate with.

Homes for Youth persona: Jasmine

Jasmine lives on the edge of Leicester with her partner and her two teenage children. She's a teaching assistant at her children's old primary school and also volunteers at a youth club at a nearby estate one evening a week. Her partner is a police officer who also volunteers at a community centre.

Jasmine doesn't get much time for reading, so doesn't buy a national daily paper but picks up a free local paper from time to time. She tries to catch the news on the TV or radio and enjoys watching natural history programmes and period dramas such as Downton Abbey.

She doesn't own her own computer but uses her daughter's laptop to Skype her sister in Australia. She also has a Facebook account where she occasionally posts photos of the family, but doesn't have a clue about Tweeting, even though her children have tried to explain it to her several times. She's heard of trolling and online bullying and is quite negative about social media. She worries about the amount of time her children spend on their computers and phones.

Jasmine recently bought a smartphone, which she uses mostly to text her family during the day. She doesn't get many emails except from work, and those she does get she usually reads in the evening on her partner's old desktop computer.

EXERCISE 8:
Developing a think/feel/do chart

Having defined your audiences, it's time to explore what you want each one to think, feel and do. Developing the different personas should have helped you get into what their interests are, what's likely to engage and motivate them, and what might stand in the way of them engaging with the organisation.

Think/feel/do charts describe different levels of engagement, first looking at the rational (think) and the emotional (feel) responses, then considering what action (do) you would like to result from your communications. This last part – the 'do' part – is important, because ultimately you could fill the world with people who agree with you or like you, but it won't mean much unless they act on it in some way.

You will also find it helpful to consider the 'barriers to engage', as well as the 'triggers to engage', since they will give you pointers as you think about the messages and tactics you use to win your audiences over.

Homes for Youth think/feel/do chart

Audience: homeless young people		
THINK/FEEL/ DO	**BARRIERS TO ENGAGE**	**TRIGGERS TO ENGAGE**
What do we want them to think?	What will stop this person engaging?	What are the motivating factors that will engage this person?
That they have a right to housing	Doesn't know help is available	Trust in organisation
That this organisation will help them find it	Concerned about confidentiality vis-à-vis parents/ family	Safe/appropriate accommodation
	Afraid of involvement with authorities, eg police	Prospect of permanent housing
		Training for employment
How do we want them to feel?	Doesn't want to give up street lifestyle	Financial support/help with benefits
That they are valued and heard	Dependent on drugs or alcohol	Chance to get off the streets
That there's a future off the streets	Peer pressure	
	How will we overcome this?	What can we do to trigger these motivating factors?
What do we want them to do?	Publicising service	Get homeless young people to tell us what they need
	Building trust	
Come along and use our services	Proving that we're safe, independent and confidential	Enable them to identify with the people we help/ have helped
Know their rights		
Kick drugs and alcohol		Provide a clear pathway for change
Return to education		

Social psychology frameworks

Social psychology and behavioural economics frameworks and theories are becoming increasingly popular in audience segmentation and insight, and they have been the source of much debate in the UK non-profit sector, particularly in the last few years.

A well-known and fairly recent entry to the conversation is 'nudge' theory, which was embraced by the coalition government, in particular as part of its strategy to improve public health. Nudge theory puts forward the idea that positive reinforcement of certain behaviours is more effective than direct instruction. It's the reason you may see more bananas placed strategically at eye level in school canteens – kids are more likely to grab one if it's in front of them than if someone tells them to seek one out. And while nudge theory's potential application in non-profit communications has been talked about, it remains largely untapped.

Some colleagues enjoy debating questions of audience attitudes and behaviours, especially which follows which. Should we aim to influence the attitudes of our audiences then expect them to behave differently as a result? Or should we play to their existing attitudes (whether or not they are aligned with ours) to persuade them to act, then expect their attitudes to change as a result of their engagement in our cause? These debates are useful and necessary but tend to blur the lines between ideology and objectivity.

Some argue that campaigns that push for action at any cost entrench negative stereotypes of our beneficiaries, and ultimately add to the problem charities exist to solve. The example of this that has been with us for years is the commonly held view that 'flies in eyes' representations of extreme poverty – which show people as powerless victims stripped of dignity – can be effective in engaging donors and the media, but may create counterproductive or distorted perceptions of the developing world.

Others argue that it's neither realistic nor desirable to expect our communications strategies to challenge or change our audiences' values – asking the question, "Is it really the role of the non-profit sector to tell people what to think or demand that their engagement is motivated by the 'right' attitudes or a shared ideology?"

Obviously the points are simplified and polarised here for clarity. But issues such as this are likely to come up in some form in the course of your work and you may need to grapple with them when developing your communications strategy. Thinking through these questions will help you find your organisation's 'ethical compass' with respect to marketing and communications, and define the boundaries.

The broad consensus among the people we consulted is that no single framework can be exclusively or wholly true, and there's really no need to be monotheistic about all of this. But it's useful to understand something about these different approaches. They will help stimulate your thinking and develop a perspective that works for your organisation. If you work with an agency, you also may find that they subscribe to one or other of these approaches.

A few frameworks

The Common Cause Project (http://valuesandframes.org) argues for an approach that cultivates audiences' values and frames (see PIRC case study below).

Cultural Dynamics Strategy & Marketing (www.cultdyn.co.uk) advises organisations on the implications of changes in cultural and individual values on policies, processes and procedures (see RSPB case study below).

Mindspace (www.instituteforgovernment.org.uk/publications/mindspace) is a highly practical behavioural economics framework that identifies the universal motivating factors (eg incentives, salience and messengers) that influence behaviour.

CASE STUDY: **PIRC and Waste Watch: Finding Common Cause**

Elena Blackmore, Public Interest Research Centre (PIRC)

Psychologists, advertisers and politicians have long understood that we are not rational, and even the most scientific or logically minded of us are influenced by values and emotions. Marketers use this knowledge to sell products, such as appealing to our desire for status in selling cars or hedonism when selling holidays.

When selling a particular product to a mass audience, this approach works well, but when the objective is broader – as with social and environmental issues – problems arise. When we appeal to a particular value, we don't simply affect a purchase decision; we also strengthen those values, and in turn influence people's social and environmental behaviour.

The research behind Common Cause, a cross-third sector social change project, shows that speaking to our 'consumer' or 'market' identity suppresses our 'civic' or 'community' identity. This means that using transactional language or appealing to self-interested goals, such as financial benefit, status and image, erodes our social and environmental concern, our long-term thinking, our civic motivation and our wellbeing. Such communications make us more materialistic and less likely to act environmentally, volunteer or be politically motivated.

Published in August 2013, our report, *Common Cause for Nature*, used original analysis on the communications of 13 UK conservation organisations to investigate what values they were appealing to.

We found that appeals to the values behind social and environmental concern – known as intrinsic values – were rare. Examples include: "Nature is amazing – let's keep it that way" and "I know that you share our vision of a future in which people and nature thrive alongside one another."

Our consumer identities – our extrinsic values – were regularly evoked. We were told we could "save nature" while we shopped and offered 10% discounts as if the natural world were any other consumer good.

The analysis also showed that the communications failed to connect with the 'social' part of intrinsic concern. This might not be surprising, given that they were talking about environmental issues, but it reflects a wider misconception that the public responds to messages in strict silos such as this. In fact, our civic identity encompasses both environmental and social values, and appealing to either of these spills over into concern about the other.

So what might environmental communications look like if they were aimed at encouraging us to develop our intrinsic, civic side?

Waste Watch – Our Common Place

'Our Common Place' is an attempt to connect the dots between different intrinsic values. Swamping community residents with ever more information on the benefits of recycling was neither effective nor inspiring. Waste Watch (now part of Keep Britain Tidy) decided to do something more community-focused.

First, it convened a series of meetings in the areas it worked in to discuss the communities' values. It found a surprising degree of consistency in responses: people said they valued family, fairness, safety, friends, music, fun and outdoor space. Next it discussed what communities would like to see more of in their area and supported communities in making those things happen. Finally, it integrated recycling messages into these activities (games based on recycling at community festivals, for instance). So how did this campaign reflect the principles of Common Cause?

- **Finding out where people 'are'**
  Almost everyone prioritises intrinsic values over extrinsic (community or family over money or image), which was brought to the fore in people's own contexts (asking them in their own communities, in this instance).

- **Engaging intrinsic values**
  Our civic identity can be encouraged through talking to associated values and avoiding appealing to the extrinsic values that suppress civic concern. Waste Watch engaged these values simply by eliciting the communities' own.

- **Participatory and inclusive**
  The bottom-up approach of working directly with the audience embodies the intrinsic values of equality, community and self-direction, and therefore encourages these values in the participants too. As expected, a number of social and community indicators improved, such as feelings of connection, cohesion and wellbeing. And recycling also increased: bins were up to 76% full (up from 60%) and contamination levels were down.

CASE STUDY: **RSPB: Using values modes**

Karen Rothwell, former director of
marketing, RSPB

Support from private individuals is vital to the RSPB's
conservation mission. They provide over 70% of the charity's
income and the one million who are members give powerful
back-up to its advocacy work. Supporter recruitment and
retention are therefore vital to the RSPB's success, which
means that understanding what motivates people is key.

For years, we recruited people into focus groups using all the
best-practice market research techniques – geo-demographic
profiling, newspaper readership, stated interest in nature or
conservation, attitudes to recycling – anything that looked like it
would draw out the people most likely to support our work. And
for years, we found ourselves observing groups of people that
included some who were absolutely on the right wavelength and
some who absolutely were not. We were missing something.

That is, until a campaign strategist introduced us to Cultural
Dynamics Strategy & Marketing (CDSM), which identifies
the different sets of values and motivators at play in any
population. It recognises three distinct groupings within the
population based on distinct underlying beliefs, values and
motivations. These are:

- Settlers – primarily motivated by safety, security
  and belonging

- Prospectors – motivated by esteem of others and
  self-esteem

- Pioneers – motivated by the aesthetic, cognitive and
  self-actualisation.

Within each of these main groups are four sub-sets, and
people tend to move through the groups as the needs of each
stage are met. To determine which group a specific individual
belongs to, CDSM uses a set of questions honed over 25
years of large-scale quantitative research. We felt these
'emotional' discriminators helped us identify common groups
in a way that the 'rational' socio-demographics had largely
failed to do, so set out to test their application to the RSPB's
communications work.

We started with a questionnaire and telephone survey to find out
the values of current supporters and designed a member appeal

with a strongly 'Pioneer' perspective to reflect the majority value group within our supporters. It was an enormously successful appeal, delivering a strong emotional impact.

On the strength of this and other testing, we 'immersed' all fundraising and communications staff in the theory, its evidence and, most importantly its application, with a workshop that helped staff imagine themselves into the different groups and design products and propositions that would appeal to their 'temporary' values state.

As we began brand positioning work for the 2007–12 strategy, we were confident enough to embed 'values modes' fully in the process. For the market research that would inform strategic decisions on RSPB's positioning and proposition, we recruited focus group attendees using the CDSM questions, so that each group included only a single values group.

At last, the focus group discussions entered an extraordinary depth of discussion as 'common mind sets' were confident to explore beliefs and attitudes that seemed to be shared by the whole group. The insights gained from these groups was clearer and deeper than we could have hoped for, showing unequivocally that each of the main values groups would be motivated to support RSPB's work by distinct approaches.

This led us to grapple with one of the key questions of application: whether to focus on just one values group, develop three sub-brands to reach all three groups, or ensure that there are triggers for all three groups in any one communication or brand proposition. Different organisations will choose different answers; the RSPB chose the last approach to reflect its broad reach.

Brand road shows carried the values modes to all staff within the RSPB, and the approach was instrumental in shaping campaigns of that period and in the strapline 'a million voices for nature'.

Three things made values a hit within the RSPB:

1. The RSPB is a science-based charity and the scientists could see that this was an evidence-based approach underpinned by robust quantitative research.

2. The simple truth of the three groups is visible and easy to experience once you have the simple framework.

3. It worked. RSPB increased membership from one million to 1.5 million in the five years it was using the CDSM methods.

Action points from Chapter 4

- Find out who your current audiences are and what they know about your organisation and the issues you work on.

- Use audience research segmentation tools to discover who your new audiences could be.

- Decide what you want them to think, feel and do, and what would motivate them to engage with you.

- Look at some social psychology frameworks and consider if any of them could work for you.

5

Setting brand goals

'Brand' is a word that gets used – and misused – a lot in this sector. But the history of the word tells us everything we need to know about what 'brand' is really supposed to be. It's a concept stolen straight from farming, where cattle are branded to distinguish them from the animals in the neighbouring field. In that context a brand wouldn't be much use if it was the same as that of the herd next door.

By their very definition then, brands must be different from each other and must tell people something about the quality of the thing they are attached to.

The purpose of your brand in communications and marketing isn't much different: your brand both marks you out and tells your audiences something unique and valuable about what you do and why you do it. But brand and communications aren't one and the same, and in this chapter we'll explore some of the differences and how to make your communications strategy and brand strategy support each other to your advantage.

Most communications strategies include objectives relating to the organisation's brand, usually increasing awareness, building brand preference or repositioning, or all three. So your communications strategy is likely to say something about the role your brand plays in supporting your aims and include goals that explain what you want to achieve for the brand.

The difference between a brand strategy and a communications strategy

For some organisations, brand strategies and communications strategies are effectively the same thing, and their communication strategies talk about raising awareness and not much else. However, in most cases this approach is too limiting as it underplays the role of communications, which has a lot of other things to do besides building brand awareness. Our advice is to make your communications strategy work harder than just waving a flag and making yourself famous. Try to think in more tangible terms about what your communications are trying to achieve, and give something of real value to your audiences. Do that and they will grow to love you all on their own.

So let's draw a distinction between brand and communications strategies. Here, we're working with the following definitions:

Brand strategy is an articulation of your organisation's positioning and personality, and how it expresses its values. It explains what's unique about your organisation and how people benefit from engaging with you. Your brand strategy probably won't include much detail on how you are actually going to get out into the world and engage people. It's a more conceptual framework that guides your communications strategy and should ideally guide other strategies, for fundraising, HR, policy and so on.

Communications strategy tells you who your organisation wants to communicate with, how and why. It's likely to include an objective to strengthen or refocus your brand, but some of your communications may have little or nothing to do with achieving brand goals at all. For example, you might choose to partner with other organisations to gain influence on a certain issue, operating under a campaign banner with limited brand presence for the individual organisations. In this situation your brand has a very limited role.

Other parts of your communication strategy may help build your brand, but have other specific aims. For example, a communication objective to persuade people to leave their car and walk to work will primarily be about achieving behaviour-change goals. If your brand is behind the campaign, it might make it more effective. Conversely, the campaign may strengthen your brand, but in this situation the brand goals are secondary and you will measure success by the number of people walking to work.

Do you have a brand strategy?

If you do, it will make the work in this chapter more straightforward. If you don't, you need to develop one. A lot of good words have been published about brand strategy in the non-profit sector, particularly CharityComms' Best Practice Guide, *Branding Inside Out*. The best of what's written focuses on the 'content' of brand development – understanding the idea of brand as being 'beyond logo' and looking at values, personality, reputation, positioning, and so on.

Increasingly, brand consultancies working in the non-profit sector have tended to focus on the intangible benefits of brands – the tonal qualities, values, and the feeling that brands engender. This is sometimes at the expense of addressing the tangible benefits of brands, the real-world stuff such as what do you do, what issues do you campaign on, or what can you do for me? Both tangible and intangible benefits are vital in brand strategy, but the 'what we do' part should not be undervalued. This is particularly true for smaller charities without big advertising budgets who depend on news, PR and social media to get their message out, because through these channels you will become known first by what you do and your position on particular issues.

It's much easier of course to get internal agreement on the intangible stuff (eg you are an authoritative brand or a challenger brand), than to agree to build your brand around one specific aspect of your work at the expense of another. To identify yourself as a challenger brand does have real meaning and can be a great position to occupy. But if you avoid decisions about what you are actually going to talk about then a piece of the puzzle is missing.

This apparent over-emphasis of intangible benefits may be borrowed from parts of the private sector – for example, financial services or fast-moving consumer goods, where it can be difficult to differentiate on the 'what we do' question. Take, for example, credit cards. Most are more or less the same in functional terms, and so the market has segmented itself less by tangible benefits such as interest rates, but by the intangible benefits or the values they are associated with. So, if we asked you to think about credit cards and write down the name of 'the posh one', 'the cool one', 'the executive one' and 'the traditional one', you could probably do that quite easily. Credit cards have little choice but to 'dial up' their intangible benefits. But charities don't have to rely on that alone. Charities do great work, have valuable information and an interesting point of view about the world – and that's what people want to hear about.

Here we are going to look at the role of brand in the context of your communications strategy to help you define and articulate the following:

- How will your brand support communications goals?

- How will your communications strategy help build the brand?

Once you have answered these questions, you will be ready to set brand goals. It will also help you decide whether your brand strategy – if it exists – is up to the job or whether it needs to be revised.

How will your brand support communications goals?

Usually your brand will have one main job: to make people more likely to choose your organisation. Despite the reams of papers and essays written on the subject, it really does boil down to this simple idea: your brand drives choice. That may be in a very obvious sense – for example, a donor choosing to give you money (and by implication, not to a competitor) – or in a less obvious sense, such as a policy adviser accepting your argument over another. So in order to figure out the role of your brand, you will need to understand the main factors that influence your audiences in making these choices. To put it another way: if you want to influence somebody's choices, you need to know a) who you are trying to influence, b) what factors they consider when making choices, and c) the extent to which your brand is a deciding factor.

Human beings make choices on the basis of complex interplays of rational and emotional drivers, and these factors will be different in each context. It's easy to overthink this, but giving it some consideration, using insight from your audience research, will be invaluable in shaping your communications strategy.

Two examples

You work for a humanitarian organisation and a journalist wants to write a story about an ongoing food crisis. If she has a strong awareness of your brand she is significantly more likely to return your calls, not only for the obvious reason that you are the first organisation she thought of, but also because she knows you will lend weight to her story by providing an authoritative, independent and reliable voice that her readers are familiar with. So your brand strength is a significant driver of choice in this situation. But it's not the only one. This journalist will also value other factors, such as your ability to respond quickly and give her what she needs (which is vital in a rapidly unfolding story), as well as the strength of your existing relationship.

Now you have switched jobs and you work for a national children's services charity. Your organisation is making a major funding application to a government body. The people evaluating your application may be reassured to have heard of you and may already have a positive impression of your services, but they are working to a strict framework, and the quality of your application and its alignment to their strategic aims are far greater factors in deciding whether or not to fund your programme. In this situation, your brand strength is not a major driver of choice – although if you are not well known, you may have to work a little harder to prove you have a solid track record.

Of course, at a certain level, your brand is for everyone – or at least all your external and internal audiences – and it's important to achieve consistency across all your communications around what you do, what you stand for and what makes you different. If you don't, you will confuse people and make yourself vulnerable to criticism.

But for your communications strategy, knowing where your brand will have the greatest influence and impact will help you figure out where to focus your brand-building efforts to achieve the greatest value in support of your communications aims. You can't be everything to all people, and the organisations that have successfully built their brands have done so with this clarity of purpose around who the brand is for.

We need to think beyond profile and ask why we want to raise profile, which leads to the question 'What's the role and value of our brand?'.

Victoria Shooter, National Deaf Children's Society

EXERCISE 9:
Who does your brand need to engage?

Try this simple exercise. As with all the exercises in this book, it's intended to prompt discussion and thinking, rather than being a scientific formula making decisions for you. We recommend trying it out with a group of colleagues and seeing where the discussion takes you. If you involve people who have expertise with specific audiences, you will reach more reliable conclusions and get a shared understanding of who your brand needs to engage. And if you have real data to populate your table, such as research findings into your audience motivations, all the better.

1. In the first column, write down your priority audiences.

2. In the second column, write down what choice you want to influence. Look back at your 'think/feel/do' charts and use the 'do' part.

3. In the third column, assign this audience a priority level (how important they are to your overall strategy) by distributing 100 points between them.

4. In the fourth column, consider how large a factor your brand is in driving choice with this audience, and again, share 100 points between them.

5. Now multiply the scores in the third and fourth columns and enter the number into the fourth column. This gives you your index.

EXAMPLE: Homes For Youth – who is your brand for?

AUDIENCE	CHOICE	PRIORITY	DRIVES CHOICE	INDEX
Policy makers and close circle of influence	Accept our arguments	20	x 5	= **100**
ABC1 mothers of teenage children	Donate to us	30	x 40	= **1200**
Broadsheet and broadcast journalists	Take our stories	20	x 25	= **500**
Vulnerable young people	Seek our help	30	x 30	= **900**

In this example, we've judged that individual givers (ABC1 mothers with teenage children) are going to be the priority for brand development. This is because they are a priority audience for Homes for Youth and brand is a key factor in whom they choose to donate to. This is a conclusion that many charities with a significant mass-market fundraising function come to.

Meanwhile, in this specific scenario we've judged that policy makers score low, because Homes for Youth has good long-lasting personal relationships in Whitehall, and the quality of any individual policy and research work is by far the over-riding factor in driving choice, with who it's from mattering less.

Homes for Youth has an interesting challenge. It needs to develop and grow a brand reputation that will both inspire people to donate and motivate youth to access its services. Reaching this conclusion will enable Homes for Youth to consider how to position the organisation to be as motivating as possible to both individual givers and service users, and in turn, which of its communications objectives will benefit most from a strong brand. Furthermore, if the board is in the mood to invest in brand building, the Homes for Youth communications team can tell them where it should be focused.

Of course, this is a fictional example, and different organisations look different on a chart like this. Those who are strongly dependent on local authority funding, for example, may prioritise their reputation as an effective local service provider in their brand development, particularly if they are in a competitive sector with other organisations bidding for the same contracts. On the other hand, for a national pressure group that uses public petitions to press for policy change, its reputation in Westminster may be the number one priority because its strategy relies on ministers believing the organisation can mobilise popular support.

Think about how this will work for you. What job does your brand need to do to deliver your communications aims and with which audiences is it likely to make the most impact? If you don't already have a brand strategy that tells you how to express your organisational values, benefits and unique selling points, you can start with the insights you have come up with here and develop something now.

Setting goals for your brand

Having identified where you will get the most value from your brand engagement, your next challenge is to set some specific brand goals. We want to look beyond general awareness objectives and set goals in line with more specific communications aims, as we explored in the previous section.

Examples of brand goals might be:

- Increasing propensity to support your charity among potential and existing individual donors
- Repositioning your organisation to achieve greater influence in particular service or policy areas
- Building trust with service users in order to improve reach into specific target groups.

The more specific your brand goals, the more useful they will be and the easier it will be to show impact.

We don't have a generic 'raise awareness' objective – all of our awareness raising work is explicitly linked to an organisational objective, so we know what we're raising awareness of and why. We may measure ourselves against communications metrics like awareness – but it will always be linked to an objective. For example: raising awareness with transplant centres in order to strengthen our customer base.

Richard Davidson, Anthony Nolan

Brand measurement

Brand measurement is usually done at four levels, often illustrated in a pyramid like this:

Action
that demonstrates your audiences have engaged with you

Propensity
to engage with your organisation in some way, including preference of your organisation over others

Understanding
of who you are and what you do

Awareness
of your organisation

Comprehensive brand measurement usually tracks all of these levels, sometimes more. The trick is to find correlations between them. For example, does propensity to support your brand actually result in action?

Brand measurement can be done with the general public (via an omnibus survey) or among more targeted or specialist audiences.

Brand awareness is usually measured in terms of:

- Unprompted awareness ("Please name every charity you have heard of")

- Semi-prompted awareness ("Please name every homelessness charity you have heard of")

- Prompted awareness ("Have you heard of Homes for Youth?").

The level of prompting relevant to your organisation will depend on a number of factors. For example:

- How well-known you are: If you are not well-known, you are unlikely to show up in an unprompted poll. Whereas if you are one of the 10 or so best-known charities, you are unlikely to move your prompted awareness figures (which will probably be over 90%), so you will be more interested in unprompted awareness, which will show how strong your brand is at any given time.

- What your specific brand challenge is: For example, if you have a long heritage but have recently been inactive, you may be more interested in addressing semi-prompted awareness, which will tell you how 'front of mind' you are.

Measuring understanding and perception of your organisation will help you understand whether you are achieving your positioning aims: that is, your audiences' understanding of what you do in terms that matter for you. This can be:

- What you do (eg what sector you are in and whether you are in service delivery or campaigning, and so on)

- The approach you take, often measured through testing positioning statements such as 'a compassionate friend', 'a technical expert' or a 'fighter for justice'

- More general value propositions which can be benchmarked against other non-profit organisations in your sector, eg trusted, effective, honest, passionate and so on.

Propensity to engage with your organisation is usually measured through questions such as:

- Which three of these 10 charities are you most likely to support (or trust, etc)?

- Do you intend to donate to (or engage otherwise with) this charity in the next 12 months?

Actions are likely to be your ultimate brand goals. The bad news is that they are the hardest to measure. But you should try, if at all possible, to show how your brand strength results in real people doing real things.

Measuring actions on their own is not the hard part. They can be measured with a range of indicators, such as the number or profile of new donors, or channel-specific measurements such as web traffic and conversion. Depending on your existing arrangements, you may need to establish new systems for measuring impact, such as attributing a policy change to your campaign or counting the number of people accessing your services. Some organisations still don't do this systematically.

The hard part will be attributing these outcomes to your brand-building activity, and usually this can only be done by spotting trends and being a little patient. If you look at sector-wide data (for example, brand strength versus voluntary income) you may be able to predict how a stronger brand preference will uplift fundraising performance. Or if you are trying to increase service uptake, you could look at historical data and project your graph forward at a sharper angle. At first, projections like this will be useful as hypotheses to track over time, but before long you should be able to identify trends and claim some credit for all of your hard work.

When you can't do it all

If you have limited capacity to measure your brand and you decide you can only look at one thing, it's usually more useful to understand your audiences' propensity to engage with you (for example, through donating) rather than simply their awareness of you. This tells you something about how effectively you are influencing choice which, after all, is what your brand is about.

Digital technologies are making brand measurement cheaper for those with low budgets and high ingenuity. Ad hoc opinion polling is getting cheaper and there are various free resources you can use such as keyword searches in Google Analytics, or tracking your Klout score to see how influential you are in the Twitter community.

If I had a dream budget, I'd like to be able to measure brand awareness, etc. Instead at LASA we did some qualitative and online research with audiences we knew and that we could manage ourselves. It's also about 'gut feel'. For example, after sharpening our brand, we knew that we were getting new partnerships and relationships that we wouldn't have done before. Brand is also about confidence inside the organisation – the brand helped all of us own and tell our story.

Zoe Amar

CASE STUDY: National Trust: An approach to brand metrics

Andrew McLaughlin, assistant director of communications, National Trust

Over the last five years we've been steadily evolving how we measure the impact of our marketing communications. We've been moving away from looking at channel outputs in isolation towards more integrated measures focused on our brand. These brand measures look at what people think, feel or do as a consequence of our activity. Importantly, we build our strategic objectives for campaigns, teams and individuals around them.

For the last three years, our Insight team has been working with Consumer Insights on our brand tracker. This is a weekly online survey that asks a vast range of questions about the Trust and the areas we work in. It goes to 110 people each week, and over the course of weeks we develop a clear and robust picture of how our brand is performing. We also have a standard set of 'golden questions' that help us identify how respondents fit within our target audience groups.

Through our brand tracker, we are able to work out how well different campaigns land with our audience segments and also what it makes them think and feel about us as a consequence. In evaluating our campaigns we are able to combine these brand metrics with other business outcomes to give a clear and rounded picture of how well we have done and where we need to make improvements.

We also use the brand tracker as a strategic measurement tool. We have developed headline brand KPIs around brand awareness, warmth and relevance. With a corporate strategy to grow our membership base, we know that boosting our warmth and relevance to supporters is key to helping them 'hop over' to become members.

Over the last year we've learned that, despite some good progress, shifting these headline KPIs is challenging. So we've dug into this some more with focus groups run by a research agency. These have helped us better understand the levers we need to pull from a marketing communications point of view to help people move from being supporters to members. As a result we'll be able to adapt our brand measures in a way that will help us be even clearer about the contribution we are making. Through our learning, we'll be able to stick with this approach for longer, too, which is important if we're thinking about the long-term evolution of our brand.

The focus on brand metrics has played an important role in how we have developed our communications strategy to reflect the overall needs of the brand. We've already seen a much tighter focus to some of our major campaigns. It's enabled us to test our brand proposition in a broader way, but it's also prompted us to look at how we are working on a day-to-day basis. We are working in a much more integrated fashion with marketing and digital colleagues, and making much smarter use of content across our paid, owned and earned channels.

It's still work in progress, but it feels as though we have a strong platform that will serve us well into the future.

Action points from Chapter 5

- Decide who your brand is for, and the role of your brand in supporting your communications aims.

- Likewise, consider how your communication strategy will help build your brand.

- Set goals for your brand, and decide how you're going to measure its impact.

- If you don't already have a brand strategy, you should probably develop one. There are lots of existing resources to help you do that (and we've listed some at the end of this guide).

6

Message development

Let's go back to our analogy of the person behind the door (see Chapter 4). Only now we know who they are, what they care about and how they like to interact with the world, so we can feel confident about talking to them on their level.

There's just one problem: there are other people on our side of the door that need to talk to them, too. So how do you make sure the various messages are coherent rather than confusing or, worse, contradictory?

Part of the job your strategy needs to do is give guidance to you and your colleagues on how to communicate your issues and talk about your organisation. That's where key messages come in, and this section offers some observations and then a framework to help you develop them.

Developing and maintaining a set of agreed messages is one of the most valuable contributions you, as a communications head, can make. If you get this right, your communications will be more impactful, because they will be more coherent and will continually remind your audiences about:

- The issues that matter

- Why they should care

- What you do and your impact

- What you are asking from them

Developing key messages

Your task here is to think about the key messages that will underpin your work, which individual communications projects will continually seek to reinforce. To be clear, your key messages are not campaign slogans or advertisement copy. They may not be used verbatim, but will act as a blueprint or core script to be used and re-used in general communications, and form part of the brief for individual campaigns. You will need to refresh and renew them from time to time to keep up with changes in your organisation and the world around you. Our advice is to develop messages with a shelf life of around 12 months, re-launching them every year within the organisation alongside your annual plan.

Some of your key messages will talk about your organisation (for example, explaining your mission, your approach and how you are funded). These will reinforce your positioning, provide important information to your audiences, and help you to explain the unique difference you make.

Other messages will hone in on the issues your organisation campaigns about or the services you provide for your beneficiaries. When you talk about issues, think about the problems in the world you are addressing and the solutions that you bring and that you are calling for. It's a good discipline to use this 'problem/solution paradigm' when talking about any of your issues, because it will make your communications sharper and more purposeful. Framing your issues in this way also forces you to root your communications in the real world because, fundamentally, you are saying that you exist to solve a problem that everyone should care about.

You are not the story

If you take just one thing away from this guide, this is a good contender: you are not the story. As outlined earlier, the job of communications is not to lift the lid on your organisation and tell everyone about everything you do; it's deciding what to communicate and with whom, to deliver the greatest impact. How many people are wandering around right now wishing they knew more about you? Probably not many. So simply telling people what you do isn't fulfilling a need that they have.

Instead, try to find something to say about the world that is interesting and relevant to your audiences, then put yourself in the story. If you work for Homes for Youth, maybe you want to start by telling your audience about the lack of affordable housing and the impact that's having on young people – why it matters right now and why your audience should care. Now you have their interest – you have made it matter – and they are ready to hear about Homes for Youth and what you plan to do about youth homelessness. Few communicators do this really well but we urge you to be one of them.

Start with your beneficiaries and the challenges they face, have the confidence to position yourself as the solution, then step back a little. Your organisation's story will be told through the stories you tell. This is particularly important in the context of your media work, because journalists won't be interested in your organisation per se, and there's no chance they will print your mission statement. What they want to know is whether you can help them talk about something that's happening in the world. Indeed, if journalists ever do start showing a keen interest in your organisation, it's unlikely to be for good reasons, and it may be a good moment to convene your crisis team – quickly.

What will motivate your audience?

All communications should motivate audiences to engage in some way, so it follows that you should be audience-centred when developing your messages. Think about the factors that will motivate them. How would you frame your issues to create engagement? How expert is your audience? What are their goals and how can you help them achieve them? Use your 'think/feel/do' charts and consider what messages are going to achieve the response you need. Think about some of the social psychology frameworks mentioned earlier and use them to explore a number of different possibilities. When developing messages, the Institute of Government's Mindspace framework is useful, because it reminds us to consider a wide range of possible motivations, including:

- Incentives – what's in it for me or what could I miss out on?

- Salience – does this feel relevant here and now? Is it current or local?

- Reinforcing social norms – everyone does this, so I should too

It's usually a bad idea to assume your audience agrees with you or cares about your issues. This is the case even if you are fighting the most just and unarguable cause, since assuming agreement can result in dull, unengaging communications, or worse, make you sound sanctimonious and preachy. Think about the popular maxim used by public speakers, filmmakers and novelists: 'Make me care'. They know that unless they hook their audiences in the first few moments, they have failed.

The people you communicate with may have given very little thought to your cause and are being bombarded every week with messages from other charities competing for attention. Others may have peculiar or uninformed views that you haven't anticipated, or they may just be uncomfortable thinking about your cause. In any case, it's your job to win them round. Keep this in mind and you are likely to produce far more persuasive communications.

What words should we use?

The bane of every good communicator's life is technical jargon. It creeps up on you, smuggled into every conversation and email, and before you know it, you have started using it too. This guide is probably full of it, but in the context of external communications – in particular, with respect to non-expert audiences – jargon won't cut it, and you will have to do your best to rid yourself of it.

A good place to start is your audience research. What words and phrases did the respondents use to describe your organisation and the issues you work on? When you are searching for that perfect phrase or a plain English translation of a technical term, your eureka moment may come in a telephone interview or focus group, from someone who doesn't know your organisation well. Often, people external to your charity will possess a clarity of thought about your issues that's difficult to hold onto for long when you are on the inside. So, however clumsy or naïve their phrasing may sound to your expert ear, you should value their perspective because they may be speaking a language that will help you connect with people like them.

In searching for accessible language, you may encounter a little resistance from expert colleagues. Sometimes there is good reason to use technical terminology – for example, with certain types of health information – and, of course, language can bring political connotations too. But you do have a responsibility to your audiences to fulfil the basic courtesy of being accessible and easy to understand.

One practical step you can take is developing a lexicon for your organisation, listing plain language equivalents of technical terms, and getting it approved by colleagues. This can help avoid arguments later and give you standardised terms to ensure consistency in your work.

CharityComms has two free Best Practice Guides which provide useful tips here. *Show and tell*, a guide to portraying beneficiaries and service users talks about the decisions you need to make about the language you use to describe your beneficiaries. And *Perfect pitch* is a Best Practice Guide to tone of voice and brand language. If you are communicating in English, it's worth reading one of the 'How to' guides from the Plain English Campaign. See the Resources section on p151 for details.

Modifying messages for different audiences

You will probably find it necessary to develop different messages for different audience groups. For example, the messages that will motivate individual donors are likely to be different from those that will motivate policy makers or beneficiaries. However, if you do this, make sure your different messages don't conflict. A common example is where fundraising messages argue that the 'solution' is increased funding for your projects, while campaign messages make the case that changes in policy and practice are needed to make a real and lasting impact. Both may be right – and it's easy to understand why each would make their case – but, as a communicator, can you reconcile these two positions in a more universal idea that will make sense to your audiences? A message such as "Governments need to act, but until they do, we'll continue working to meet the needs of the most vulnerable" certainly achieves it.

Your overarching messaging framework

The framework below illustrates the areas you will need to consider when you develop your key messaging. There is no single approach, and every communications head we consulted addressed this challenge a little differently, so you will need to find the approach that works best for you.

The framework shows the different levels of messages you will need in order to create a story that makes sense, both about your organisation and about the issues you work on. The first six lines are the key messages about your organisation and will help you describe yourselves consistently. The final line (Issue 1, Issue 2, etc.) is where you focus on your issues and should account for most of your communications work. This is explored in the next exercise, 'Developing messages'.

WHO WE ARE			
A single sentence: what/who are we?			
OUR VISION, MISSION AND VALUES			
Briefly, the world we want to see and how we are going to get there.			
WHAT WE DO AND WHO WE DO IT FOR			
One or two sentences on what we do and who our beneficiaries are.			
CONTEXT			
Something on the political, social, economic or technological context we are operating in, to give a sense of our relevance today.			
OUR APPROACH			
What is our unique approach to addressing the rights of our beneficiaries?			
OUR SUPPORTERS AND PARTNERS			
Who supports us? Who do we partner with?			
ISSUE 1	ISSUE 2	ISSUE 3	ISSUE 4
More detailed key messages for our issues, programmes and fundraising and campaigns (see Message Matrix p100).			

EXERCISE 10:
Developing messages

Begin with the overarching message framework shown above. How would your organisation fit into this? Hopefully, you will have considered many of these areas in your discovery phase and brand development work.

This framework would never be a public document – not for reasons of secrecy, but because in this form it's probably not very interesting to your audiences. But it provides a part of the 'core script' that you and your colleagues can refer to. Having organisation-wide agreement on how you describe yourself, what you do, the context you work in, how you are funded, and so on, is a great start in achieving coherence.

This is another exercise that you could try on your own or in a workshop setting with colleagues. Either way you will need help and contributions from colleagues in some way, because you probably won't have all the information you need. And, as with all of the exercises in this guide, involving colleagues can help you get them involved in developing the strategy, and more generally 'bought in' to the need for coherent messages.

Many of the communications heads we spoke to during the research for this guide use a similar approach to message development. This approach should help you stick to the core discipline of defining a problem and a solution, and will allow you to 'put yourself in the story' as we discussed earlier. It will also remind you of the need to be clear in all communications about what you are asking from your audience. It's very rare that you would want to communicate something without asking anything from your audience, so it's a good discipline when creating messages to say to yourself, "What are we asking for here?".

Most key messages can be developed by addressing four questions:

- What's the issue?

- Why is it important now?

- What are we doing about it?

- What do we want you to do?

Each of these can be supported by proof points, a term used to describe the underlying facts, statistics and other references that 'prove' or validate your key messages. And each can be brought to life with personal stories – quotes, case studies or testimonials from your beneficiaries, supporters or staff, to bring home the 'human truths' in your messages.

We've put all of these into a 'message matrix', shown overleaf.

PROPOSITIONS	PROOF POINTS	PERSONAL STORIES...
What's the issue? A simple articulation of the problem or issue	Statistics and memorable facts to support the proposition	...that illustrate the human truths behind the issue
Why does it matter now? To create salience, urgency or a reason to engage	Facts to emphasise the urgency and seriousness of the issue	...that illustrate how it's affecting people now
What are we doing about it? To position the organisation and establish its right to talk about the issue	Information about the organisation's programme, campaigning and fundraising work	...that demonstrate how the organisation is helping people and bringing about change in their lives
What do we want you to do? Calls to action	Information about why action is needed and evidence that it works	...that show how supporter actions can help individuals

Try it now. How would you address these questions for your organisation? Can you develop a message matrix for each of your main areas of work? Perhaps you will need to produce message matrices for different levels of detail.

For example, in the case of Homes for Youth, we could write one that positions the overall strategic purpose of the organisation (tackling youth homelessness) and a range of matrices for sub-themes (for example, getting young people back into education). Or we could write messages for specific audiences like the one overleaf, which was written for supporters.

Homes for Youth message development matrix for supporter acquisition

PROPOSITIONS	PROOF POINTS	PERSONAL STORIES...
What's the issue? Youth homelessness...	80,000 young people in the UK are homeless One-third of them are living on the streets, where they are alone and vulnerable to violence and abuse	"I've been homeless since I ran away from home. I know it's dangerous and I'm scared, but I'm too scared to go back." Claudia, 17, who's been living on the streets in Birmingham for two years
Why does it matter now? ...is back on the rise, and reaching critical levels following changes to benefit laws	Youth homelessness increased by 10% last year. It's likely to go up a further 15% next year. Our research shows that benefit cuts are the main cause of this rise, both directly, because fewer young people can afford housing, and indirectly, because more families are breaking up due to financial pressures	"My parents threw me out because their benefits were cut. Most of the people I sleep rough with are younger than me and there seems to be more of them around King's Cross every day." Jake, 16
What are we doing about it? Homes for Youth provides hostel accommodation and advice services to help homeless young people to access healthcare, get back into education and find jobs	Last year we provided hostel accommodation for 1,203 young people, referred 975 for healthcare and supported 754 back into education and training for work	"I never thought I'd get any GCSEs but my Homes for Youth worker helped me get a place at an adult education college and now I'm studying maths and English." Amal, 18
What do we want you to do? All over the UK, people are joining our 'Wake up to Youth Homelessness campaign'. Please be part of it. Tweet it, Facebook it, make a donation or volunteer at one of our drop-in centres	We're facing deep cuts in our government funding, just when young people need us most If 1,000 people give £5 a month, we will keep one of our hostels open and give 45 young people a desperately needed escape from life on the streets We depend on volunteers to help get homeless young people back into education or work	"I was shocked when I found out how many young people – the same age as my own children – sleep rough every night. I just had to do something." Florence, who volunteers at a Homes for Youth drop-in centre

Dare to be simple

As you go through the process of developing your messages, you will find yourself grappling with complex questions, multiple voices with subtly different perspectives, and a lot of nuance in the issues you are working on. But as any good brand strategist will tell you, your job – the job of any communicator – is to find the simple truths at the heart of your issues and build from there.

However, as Jakob Nielsen, the web usability guru, said, "Ironically, the practice of simplicity is not simple" and you will need moments of creativity, clarity of thought and a little courage to get there.

This does not mean you should 'dumb down'. Far from it. You need to do your research, listen to your colleagues and think your subject through very carefully. But ultimately, your job is not to prove to your audiences how smart you are, it is to distil and communicate confidently in a way that will engage, inspire and persuade them to think or act differently.

As you go through this distillation, specialist colleagues will tell you it's more complicated than that, and on one level they are right. But the message, 'Poverty: it's complicated' never won a campaign and never raised any money. You need simple truths to do that, and at the core of any issue, you will find something essential: an injustice, a visceral human experience or an opportunity for change. When you find it, hang onto it and don't let go.

We use different sets of messages depending on who we're communicating with. The PR team oversees a 'key messages' document - a living document that records our key messages on any given topic in media friendly language. This saves time when briefing spokespeople or preparing statements at short notice. Fundamentally, our overarching key messages are simple: asthma is prevalent, it can kill, and we need money to fund vital research and our award winning services. Everything builds from there.

Claudine Snape, Asthma UK

CASE STUDY: Stonewall: Keeping things simple

Laura Doughty, deputy chief executive, Stonewall

It's a proud moment when any charity can point to a campaign and describe it as 'iconic'. Our 'Some People Are Gay. Get Over It!' campaign certainly seems to have earned that description. From classrooms to travel card holders, Stonewall's bold creatives have been displayed in thousands of locations and seen by millions of people across Britain and overseas since the campaign was launched in 2007.

The campaign was conceived as part of our work to tackle the appalling levels of homophobic abuse and bullying in Britain's schools. We wanted to give lesbian, gay and bisexual young people a simple message they could use to help tackle bullying. 'Some People Are Gay. Get Over It!' was suggested in a sixth-form focus group. It was concise and simple, and perfectly captured our objective.

Keeping the school audience in focus, we created a range of materials including posters, stickers and postcards that young people could use in creative ways. We worked hard to make sure the finished products looked bold and distinctive, and that young people would be proud to display them. And so they did – stickers on exercise books, posters in classrooms and postcards in libraries across Britain's schools shared our message with hundreds of thousands of young people and their teachers.

It became clear that the message could be used for other audiences and in other ways. Our most important audience outside schools was lesbian, gay and bisexual people in general. We wanted them to understand Stonewall's role in standing up for equality, and to be proud to be who they are. Pride marches were a clear opportunity, as our message was already so fundamental to those events. So we took to the streets of London for Pride wearing 'Some People Are Gay. Get Over It!' t-shirts. We were able to stage photoshoots with celebrities like Sir Ian McKellen and the then-X Factor judge, Dannii Minogue, wearing the shirts, generating interest beyond the LGB audience and into the general public. Our pop culture work continued, with Celebrity Big Brother winner Rylan Clarke and his X Factor co-contestant Lucy Spraggan also modelling the t-shirt.

To get the message out to an even bigger audience, we focused on real broadcast opportunities: transport advertising and billboards. Bus ads, in particular, enable us to take the message to high streets and village greens across the country. We've run several national campaigns and each time we reach new audiences and get new reactions. We work hard to extend the street campaign to social media, increasing exposure and opening an opportunity for dialogue with potential supporters. Increasingly, we've noticed the campaign being mentioned on social media, even outside our main campaign cycle.

Social media is a great place for this kind of campaign to take off, but it works well even in more established media. Twice in 2012 we hit the papers when we ran the campaign on buses. If imitation is the sincerest form of flattery, we can be proud that a profoundly anti-gay organisation adapted our campaign to read 'Not Gay, Ex-Gay and Post-Gay. Get Over It!'. When the Mayor of London stepped in to prevent this offensive message about nonsense 'gay cure therapy' appearing on London buses, our campaign picked up a huge amount of positive sentiment and appeared in a six-minute *Channel 4 News* story.

The campaign's success lies in its simple message and format, both of which are easily adapted to speak to new audiences for new campaigns. 'Some People Are Bi. Get Over It!' spoke to the bisexual community, and our 'Some Girls Marry Girls. Get Over It!' (or guys) campaign helped get our social media followers behind our campaign for equal marriage. It's a format that works well for us every time.

Looking back, three simple campaigning principles are evident to us. Keeping a message simple, developing a solid understanding of your audiences, and being endlessly creative with how you reach them are fundamental to developing a good campaign strategy. It's already worked for us and will work well for some time to come.

Action points from Chapter 6

- Develop central key messages that will motivate and inspire your audiences.

- Remember, you are not the story – it's the people you work with and the issues they face that your audiences are interested in.

- Develop a messaging framework, with different levels of messages that can be used as a core script to make it all hang together.

- Keep it simple, not because you want to dumb down but because what your organisation does is fundamentally simple.

7

Channel planning

By now you will have most of the essential building blocks for your communications strategy.

You should know:

- What you want to achieve and a broad direction for your communications function

- Who you want to communicate with and what you want them to think, feel and do

- How your brand is going to help achieve that

- What your key messages are going to be – at least for the first year

Hopefully, you will have brought your colleagues along with you, not only having some great contributions from them, but also persuading them that your communications strategy is going to help them achieve positive and transformative impact.

Your task now is to consider which channels you should use to reach your audiences.

What do we mean by channels? The term is used to describe the routes you are going to take to reach your audiences. Are you going to use news media, the website, publishing or social media? Probably all of these and more besides. These are your channels and knowing how to organise them and understanding the different functions they play in your strategy is an important part of the picture. Channel planning tells you how you are going to deliver communications to achieve your goals by the most effective and efficient route possible.

PR agencies and media planners typically organise channels into three groups with distinct characteristics: bought, earned, and owned media. We've added a fourth, social media, since it behaves differently from the others.

- **Bought media**

  Advertising and marketing channels that you pay for, including TV, radio, cinema, outdoor, press advertising, direct mail and online.

- **Earned media**

  News, consumer PR and other editorial coverage mediated through journalists. This includes print, broadcast and digital channels such as high-profile blogs.

- **Social media**

  This includes social channels such as Facebook, Twitter, YouTube and countless others.

- **Owned media**

  This could include your organisational website plus any other media space over which you have full ownership and control. For example, vehicle livery, shop fronts or leaflets in service centres.

Media review

As part of your discovery phase (covered in Chapter 2), it's useful to include some research into what's happening across all these media with respect to your sector or issue. This will help you understand where the opportunities are and make an assessment of your performance in each of these channels. This is also an opportunity to look at your competitors to see how they are doing and what you could learn. Your media review can provide very specific answers about what's working for you (and what isn't), as well as data to measure yourself against, such as media reach, website traffic and social media influence.

Questions to ask include

- How much earned media space is dedicated to your issues and what's your 'share of voice' relative to your competitors' on those issues? Is there any space you can occupy? Who are the key journalists and what are the key titles most active on your issues?

- How much web traffic do you achieve compared to similar organisations? Who are your web users and what are they doing? How many of them are converting to deeper forms of engagement? Which organisations are doing the best work in this channel?

- What's happening in social media? When and where is the 'buzz' happening around your issues? Who are the main social media influencers in the blogosphere and among the Twitterati that you could target?

- What are organisations in your sector spending on bought media and how does that link to other indicators, such as brand performance or voluntary income? If you are using bought media, which channels are working best for you?

Media analysis and planning tools

There are a number of established tools for channel analysis that allow you to look in some depth at print media coverage, social media network analysis, all forms of expenditure in bought media, and many more. Directly accessing these tools can be expensive, so it's usually more cost-efficient to seek help from a communications agency, as many will have ongoing subscriptions to a range of media analysis tools.

However, if you are producing your strategy on a shoestring, there are some free and low-cost research tools available online. Spend a little time searching the web and you will find a wealth of resources. Here are a few (see our Resources section for more details):

- The *National Readership Survey* publishes free general demographic information about newspaper and magazine readership, which could help you develop a basic mapping of what your audience is reading.

- Ofcom and the Office for National Statistics both publish and update high-level demographics of internet usage.

- Alexa.com provides comparative information on website performance that could help you perform a ranking of the websites in your sector. The data is a little patchy, particularly for websites with relatively low traffic, but it could give you a reasonably reliable snapshot of how you and your competitors are performing. Comscore, a more accurate and detailed, paid-for service, gives away some data for free.

- Various free or low-cost tools such as Sprout Social offer detailed information on social media use. Some of the better tools allow you to analyse social networks, discovering the most influential people on your topic, and therefore who to target.

- Google Alerts are an excellent way of tracking news presence of issues or brands by keyword, although it's difficult to use as an archive to track, say, coverage over the past two years. You will need a paid-for service for that.

- The British Film Institute (BFI) research and statistics unit (RSU) publishes in-depth reports about demographics and attitudes among cinema-goers.

- Information on audience penetration of advertising channels tends to be more complex and difficult to get for free. However, if you are already investing in paid-for advertising or marketing channels, your agency might provide detailed demographic and usage data, and report on media 'value' (estimated spend) in your sector as part of their service. There's no harm in asking.

Start with an open mind: media-neutral planning

Some of the communication heads we consulted recommended a 'media-neutral' approach to channel planning. Indeed, most media agencies claim to take this approach. Media-neutral means that you should begin the process with an open mind and consider which channels will reach the right audience to achieve your objective.

While that may sound natural, it's rare to find people who genuinely practise media-neutral planning. More typically, we ask ourselves media-specific questions such as "What shall we publish this year?",

"What shall we put on the homepage?" or the most common of all, "What shall we tell *The Guardian* today?"

We tend to limit our thinking in this way for practical reasons – the structures and capacities we invest in. If we have a great publishing manager and a press officer with good links to *The Guardian*, we're going to want to keep them busy. This strategy development process is a perfect moment to reappraise your approach and think afresh about the right channel mix for your organisation. You may come back to a similar place, but it's worth giving this some serious thinking time as you develop your strategy.

Identifying audience touch points

Media planners often talk about channels in terms of 'touch points' and focus strongly on context when planning campaigns. For example, they might predict that certain messages will resonate with people when they are spending time with their family and others when they are at work. So they build campaign plans around scenarios and lifestyles, identifying the most effective touch points in each relevant context. Here's a commonly used exercise for identifying these touch points:

EXERCISE 11:
Scenario development

Scenario development is a popular technique you could try, that will help you to turn your thinking on its head and imagine what it's like being at the receiving end of your communications. And it helps to remind you that the world is a chaotic place, where people think about things other than your organisation and generally won't always do what you want them to. Try this exercise with your most creative colleagues, because you need people who are ready to express unexpected ideas and put themselves in the shoes of your audiences. With six to eight people, you should be able to come up with scenarios for three audience types in a half-day session.

Digital strategists often use similar exercises, and because part of their job is to analyse and optimise every transaction in great detail, they will create 'use cases' that aim to describe user interactions with real accuracy. In communications planning you can be a little freer. Here, scenario development is a technique for exploring possibilities rather than illustrating a wholly accurate situation, and so you are free to develop idealised scenarios where audiences might come across your messages countless times in any given day.

Start with the personas you developed earlier, and work with your colleagues to create a 'day in the life' for each of them, focusing on the touch points they encounter through the day. What are the moments in their day when they are likely to make decisions or change their minds? Where were they? How did they encounter your message? Did you give them an opportunity to respond? What did your message make them think, feel or do?

Then think about them one or two years later – another day in the life. What's changed?

A day in the life of Jasmine

It's one of her work days so Jasmine has to get up and leave the house before everyone else since the school where she works is further across town. She hears something on the news about the number of young homeless people having gone up again this year, but has to run to catch the bus.

She notices on the bus that there's an ad for a charity that supports homeless young people and thinks about something her husband said, that the people on the streets seemed to be getting younger and that lots of them were girls. She thinks of her own children and immediately texts them to check that they are OK and on their way to school.

At the school, the head is asking for ideas about what to raise money for at their next mufti day. Jasmine remembers the ad on the bus, but can't remember the name of the charity. She speaks up though and tells the head about the rise in youth homelessness. She says she will find out the name of the charity and email a website link.

That evening she gets her daughter to search homelessness charities and Homes for Youth comes up as a paid result in the search engine. The others don't have youth in their name, so she's sure that's the one she saw on the bus. Looking over her shoulder, her partner says he's heard of them but thought they were London-based. However, the website makes it clear that they are a national charity, with a regional office in Leicester. It also offers lots of fundraising ideas to try in school and there's a number to call a local fundraising adviser that can help set up an event.

Jasmine emails the head, suggesting they make Homes for Youth their mufti day charity, and sends a link. The head agrees to this and, after talking to the local fundraising adviser, also picks them to be their charity of choice for their Christmas appeal.

Jasmine: two years later

Jasmine's son has left home and is now going to university in London. Unable to find a room he can afford, he's staying with a cousin. Jasmine's daughter did well in her GCSEs and has decided to do sociology as one of her 'A' levels, having become concerned about issues such as homelessness through her parents' voluntary work and the people and organisations she's connected with on social media.

Cuts at Jasmine's school meant she couldn't hang onto her job, so the family is still struggling a little financially. Soon after leaving, she felt isolated and bored so she took a basic computer course. She's now an enthusiastic social networker and is considering doing an Open University degree.

Since starting the new job, Jasmine's husband has stopped doing so much front-line work, but Jasmine is still acutely aware of youth homelessness; it comes up a lot in her social networking and her son has told her that even some of his fellow students have slept rough because they can't afford London rents.

Jasmine on 'wake up to youth homelessness' campaign launch day

Jasmine no longer has to get up to go to work so she has a lie-in and listens to the Today programme on Radio 4. Apparently there's going to be a lobby of Parliament about the increasing numbers of young people being forced onto the streets because of benefit cuts. A spokesperson from Homes for Youth – which has launched a report on the subject – says that if the government doesn't reverse its policies immediately, the situation will get much worse and spread across cities throughout the country.

Jasmine gets up, makes a cup of tea and puts on the small TV in the kitchen. She sees a short appeal asking for a £10-a-month donation to Homes for Youth. She remembers the fundraising event she helped organise at the school and logs on to her computer. On the Homes for Youth site she reads some of the personal stories of young people the charity has helped. She notices that one is a young woman from Leicester who ran away to London and wonders if she was at school with her daughter, who's the same age. She feels moved by the young woman's story, which describes the dangers she faced sleeping rough and how much better her life is since Homes for Youth found her accommodation and helped her enrol on a course. She breathes a sigh of relief that both her children are safe.

Jasmine posts a link to Homes for Youth's fundraising page on her Facebook page. She decides that tomorrow she'll go into town and visit the Homes for Youth advice centre. Maybe she will start volunteering there, or find out what else she can do to support the organisation.

That evening she watches the TV news about the 'Wake Up To Youth Homelessness Day Of Action' and catches sight of her son holding a HOMES FOR YOUTH NOW! banner outside the Houses of Parliament. She feels proud of him and texts her daughter to tell her that her brother's been on the TV. Jasmine talks to her partner and together they decide to donate £10 a month to Homes for Youth.

Using your scenarios

This scenario has taught us many things: that Jasmine is strongly motivated by issues that affect her family, that it took several nudges from different touch points to get her to engage, and that Jasmine is a 'word-of-mouth influencer' and needs information to help her do that. It's interesting that the fact that Homes for Youth had a presence in Leicester was important to Jasmine, as was her husband's day-to-day exposure to the issues, which served as validation.

So, taking all of this into account, what can Homes for Youth do to encourage and support community-based fundraising and volunteering? In this case:

- A great website with practical fundraising ideas and personal stories from beneficiaries, both to deepen engagement and offer useful resources

- A strong news media presence to create a sense of salience and urgency around the issue, positioning Homes for Youth as an authoritative voice

- The possibility of personal contact with a local fundraising adviser

- Bought media in television and paid search to keep prompting for donations

- A social media presence to maintain visibility of the issue and mobilise word-of-mouth influencers.

This process of scenario development has helped us think broadly about communications and the mix of channels we need to use to help Jasmine become a committed supporter and advocate for our cause. From here, we can start our channel planning with some creative ideas about what's going to work.

Choosing your channels

Now you can start to develop a high-level plan outlining the main channels you will be using to reach your different audiences. Try laying it out in a table like this, to give yourself an at-a-glance overview, before developing a more detailed channel plan at the next stage:

Homes for Youth audiences and channels

MEDIA		AUDIENCE		
		Homeless young people	Individual supporters	Politicians & opinion leaders
EARNED	Broad-sheet press			√
	Local & regional press	√	√	
	Consumer magazines		√	
	Local & national radio news		√	√
	Local & national TV news		√	√
BOUGHT	TV		√	
	Outdoor	√	√	
	Paid search	√	√	√
SOCIAL	Facebook	√	√	
	Twitter	√	√	√
OWNED	Publishing	√		√
	Website	√	√	√

Homes for Youth channel plan

Building from the table of objectives you developed earlier, take each of your communications functions and its associated audience, and develop a new chart to show which channels will be used. Use this to note expected reach, response mechanism and some narrative to show the purpose of the channel.

In this example, we've picked the 'behaviour change' function, looking at how we can reach vulnerable young people in various ways to persuade them to communicate with their peers, keep safe, know their rights, and access Homes for Youth's services. Here's how:

Organisational objective: Young people's access to support services before they become homeless is increased

Communications function: behaviour change

Audience: Young people aged 14 to 24 who are either homeless or at high risk of becoming homeless

CHANNEL	ACTIVITY	PURPOSE	PROJECTED REACH IN YEAR 1	RESPONSE MECHANISM
Local and regional press	News stories about local youth homelessness and profiling our drop-in centres	Build trust and credibility of our services	8 million (readership)	Telephone helpline and website
Outdoor	Low-cost train station advertising promoting our services	Promote safe behaviours and build trust and general awareness of our services	2 million (footfall)	Telephone helpline and website
Facebook	Encourage peer-to-peer support and promote 'Phone a Friend' campaign	Strengthen links between peers to improve knowledge and safety	300,000 (timeline views)	Facebook message
Twitter	Establish #phoneafriend hashtag and facilitate network of homeless youth	Strengthen links between peers to improve knowledge and safety	50,000 (via Tweets); 750,000 (via reTweets)	Tweet
Publishing	Pocket-sized rights information booklets distributed through hostels and youth centres	Improve youth awareness of housing rights and increase access to our services	10,000 (readership)	Telephone helpline and website
Paid search	Pay-per-click focused on searches for short-term accommodation	Direct homeless youth to appropriate information	50,000 (clicks)	Phone or live chat
Website	Mobile-ready, user-friendly rights information and promote telephone advice service	Improve youth awareness of housing rights and increase access to our services	100,000 (unique visitors)	Phone or live chat

Things to think about

When developing your channel plan, it's worth giving consideration to the characteristics of different channels and how they work for your audience. Think about:

- **Reach – how many people will see this?**

  Probably your most important consideration. Look back at your media research to help you estimate this.

- **Focus – how targeted is this channel?**

  In the main, does it reach people in your defined target audience or those that aren't a priority for you? Less targeted channels aren't always a problem, as long as you are reaching enough of the right people, but unfocused channels are ultimately inefficient.

- **Frequency – how often will this reach its audience?**

  Media planners tend to aim to reach priority audiences eight or nine times to achieve optimum engagement. Of course, the right amount depends on who you are talking to and how attentive they are likely to be, but reaching an audience only once or twice is certainly unlikely to achieve much.

- **Level of engagement – is this a 'lean forward' or 'lean back' channel?**

  Some channels, such as radio or outdoor, provide a backdrop and people tend not to be particularly attentive. On the other hand, your website or a magazine feature will demand greater engagement and will allow you to convey more complex messages. 'Dwell time' – how long people spend engaging with a channel – is also important, which is why cross-track advertising on train station platforms is one of the few outdoor channels where you can share a lot of information.

- **Audience relationship to the channel – for example, level of trust**

  In general, people tend to trust the regional press more than the national press, because they feel connected to it in some way. Oddly, research has also indicated that people trust cinema advertising more than television advertising. User-generated content that endorses the content you are looking at can also affect your relationship to it – hence the growing trend of charities running live feeds of donations and campaign actions on their websites.

- **Context – where and when is the person likely to encounter this channel?**

  If your audience research tells you that the people you want to reach access the internet mainly at work, does that influence the kind of content you put on your website? Or if you are going to be reaching people while they are shopping, what will their frame of mind be and what might you reasonably ask them to do? There are no hard and fast rules about context, only that it's something to consider when developing your channel mix and it may prompt a few new ideas.

Different channels, different jobs

Remember the distinct job each channel has to do. News media, for example, may provide your authoritative voice and lend credibility to your message. You may decide to use your website and events as your key engagement and response channels, with poster and banner campaigns delivering emotional impact and general awareness, and paid search and social media driving traffic.

Different channels have different jobs to do. Cinema is a perfect moment for emotional engagement – you have a captive audience. But they're not going to respond. You would follow through in other channels to drive response – although you might not see immediate returns because cinema, above all, is for winning hearts and minds, not response.

Channel planning is like a graphic equaliser. Your TV ad might be the bass. Your press ad is the midrange. And the treble is provided by the event you are holding. They're all driving towards the same aim – to produce the richest, sweetest sound.

Mike Taylor, Mikeemedia

Mix it up...

Think about the interplay between channels and how they deliver different parts of your message. When audiences encounter you through more than one channel, you will generally achieve stronger engagement and trust in what you have to say. Channels reinforce each other because when audiences see something in more than one place, a sense of ubiquity is created. People think, "Ah, that's a thing that's happening in the world."

 ## CASE STUDY: Macmillan Cancer Support: Integrated channel planning

James Renwick, senior brand manager,
Macmillan Cancer Support

Macmillan's ambition is to reach and improve the lives of everyone living with cancer and inspire millions of others to do the same. Effective communications are a vital part of our brand strategy to achieve this. However, it's really important to recognise that communications can only do so much. If the experiences we deliver for customers through our services, fundraising and volunteering fall short of the brand promise that we are communicating, it can have devastating reputational consequences.

Since 2006, we have used our communications to try to shift ingrained misperceptions of people who associate us solely with end of life nursing care, rather than as an organisation that is there for everyone affected by cancer from diagnosis onwards with a wide range of support services. While our brand affinity levels are high, our communications and corporate partnerships need to work especially hard to maintain and improve awareness levels and understanding, bearing in mind we don't have Macmillan shops on the high street and because some of our services (embedded in the NHS) are less visible with limited branding opportunities.

Macmillan is here to support everyone living with and affected by cancer. This requires us to engage not just the two million people currently diagnosed with cancer, but also the 17 million family and close friends around them. And with the number of people with cancer set to rise from two to four million by 2030, there's an increasing need to broaden our reach to include as many people as possible.

This presents a significant challenge, so to ensure we really understand our primary audiences, we use a combination of qualitative and quantitative research that informs our approach to targeting and messaging. A comprehensive and continuous programme of brand health tracking provides a level of insight far richer than pure awareness measures to really get to the heart of how people feel about Macmillan.

Since 2007, we have consistently invested in brand advertising across channels including TV, radio, press, digital and outdoor. These campaigns have focused on a range of Macmillan services and have been supported by traditional and social media. In 2013, we launched a new integrated 'Not Alone' campaign, focusing on our belief that no one should face cancer alone. This marks a significant shift in our communications strategy. The campaign is still designed to address misperceptions, build understanding of Macmillan services and encourage people to get support, but crucially also to give support. We know that people who have used Macmillan services and their families often want to give something back either financially or through volunteering, so for the first time in our brand advertising we have introduced an explicit fundraising ask.

This approach is taking us on quite a journey, but is already proving effective in helping us communicate our purpose in the world in a more compelling and consistent way – whether we are communicating about our services or fundraising – and is a key building block of our brand strategy. Working in such an integrated way presents many challenges, so we're constantly testing and improving how we do things.

We use a fully integrated mix of paid, owned and earned communications channels, so it's crucial that our brand and messaging is delivered consistently across these platforms at every stage of the customer journey. This includes our corporate partner channels as well as how we engage with audiences across social media and, of course, how we behave as individuals within the organisation.

We are confident there is further potential to build our brand by inspiring and engaging a far wider audience than ever before to get involved in our cause. Adopting a fully integrated approach to our communications is key to achieving this.

Big Tactics

Your channel plan is your tool for describing in broad terms the main approaches you are going to use as you roll out your strategy. It will also help you work out what skills are needed in the team and if investment is available, where it should be directed. If you are working with good information and your channels are working hard for you then your channel plan will give your strategy focus – and help you reach the right people at the right moments.

But your channel plan doesn't tell you everything about what you are going to do. It doesn't, for example, tell you much about what the activity looks like – how you are going to use the channels. What content, what 'products' or what big ideas are you going to set in place to make your activity hang together?

- Could you achieve some of your aims by delivering information and advice to your service users through a big digital project?

- Or perhaps a yearly flagship report to establish you as a 'go-to' voice among policy makers and media, generating material for a public campaign push?

- How about a national retail partnership to give you an online and high-street 'point of sale' presence and, in doing so, strengthen your brand and recruit new supporters?

These are your Big Tactics – the three or four major projects that will bring your strategy to life and around which you will organise much of your work.

Usually strategies don't say much about tactics because they are intended to establish a broad framework, leaving tactics to be addressed in day-to-day work or through individual projects and campaigns you roll out over the strategy period.

In practice, however, your communications strategy could be significantly strengthened by including some of your boldest and most creative tactical ideas. Because without them, you can find yourself with a dry, corporate document, and some people may find it difficult to visualise what you are actually going to do.

That doesn't mean you will need to develop all of your ideas to fruition. It will probably take a little time, after your strategy is agreed, to properly weigh up all of your options and decide which

Big Tactics are going to achieve your strategic aims. But sketching out a few possibilities will give you a good starting point and bring shape to your work.

Somewhere toward the end of your strategy development process, we suggest that you hold a creative workshop with colleagues and work up a list of Big Tactics. You could think about bringing external people into this too. For example, if you work with a communications agency, they will no doubt be very happy to contribute, if it signals future work for them as you go into implementation.

Begin the session with a summary of where you currently are in your process. You know your aims, audiences, channels and key messages, so share all of this at the beginning of the meeting to keep the session on track. And share the scenarios you have developed as some of these may include elements that could spark some big ideas. Depending on how many people you involve, you could work in one or several groups. Ask them to develop two or three Big Tactics – perhaps one per communications function or audience – which they have to pitch to you, *Dragon's Den*-style, at the end of the session. Your judging criteria? Simple:

- Is this aligned with the strategy?

- Is it big enough?

- Do you believe your audiences will engage with this?

- Is it exciting? Does it give you goose bumps?

Chances are, there will be a lot of ideas already floating around in the ether which your colleagues have been desperate to share with you. Now's their opportunity.

Innovation

Your new communications strategy implies change. Of course, you are likely to continue doing some things, but having explored the possibilities and developed a shortlist of Big Tactics, you will inevitably want to start up a few new projects.

But here's the thing: most new projects fail.

Think about it this way: if you were a venture capitalist – or a *Dragon* – it's unlikely that you would put all of your expectation into just one new business idea. That would be a risky approach, particularly when you consider that around 70% of new businesses in the UK fail in their first year. Instead, what you would do is invest in a number of different businesses, and while you would do your best to make them all succeed, you would expect some to fail.

It's the same for you. As a communications director, each of your new projects is like a new business, because success or failure depends on a range of factors that are difficult to control, factors that any new business faces, such as:

- Whether your audience likes what you are offering

- Whether you can reach enough of the right people to have an impact

- Whether you can find skilled people to deliver it for you

- Whether your cash flow (budget) is strong enough to keep it going through lean times.

In fact, it's a little tougher for non-profits because most of the time you are not offering anything of direct tangible benefit to your audiences. This is the advantage that Apple Inc has over you: at the end of a transaction with them you get an iPhone. You, on the other hand, are offering something that may ultimately be more enriching – an opportunity to do something good for someone else – but is a little harder to describe and doesn't come in a nice box. Charity is a tough sell.

So as you develop your Big Tactics, think of them as a portfolio of new business ideas and try to move a few of them forward on the understanding that not all of them will survive. And if you are asking for new investment from your board, you will have a more fruitful engagement with them if you position your projects in this way. Better to ask for seed investment for three or four projects, with the expectation that perhaps two will survive, than to ask the board to invest in a single project that, according to the odds, has a good chance of bombing. This is risk management.

A few more things to consider as you develop your big tactics:

- Balance brand new ideas with ramping up of tried and tested approaches. This will help you build on existing knowledge and improve your chances of success.

- Look at what other organisations have done and learn from what has worked for them. Then use the 'second mover advantage' by improving on it.

- Above all, be sure to manage expectations in your organisation, otherwise your 'failures' will become an excuse to stop trying new things. Remember, if you manage risk well and innovate carefully, you can tackle risk aversion in your organisation.

Of course, innovation doesn't just happen when you are writing the strategy. Well-functioning communications teams are awash with new creative ideas (for most of us, the buzz we get from idea generation is why we work in communications in the first place). So you will naturally want to encourage an innovation culture among your colleagues and in your team, if you have one, to maintain that steady flow of new ideas.

Your job is to help people to share their ideas and take risks, and learn from both success and failure. If you can, try setting aside some of your budget to offer seed funding to colleagues who step forward with new ideas. If you can't invest, don't worry – organisations with scarce resources are often the most innovative. "Because we're a small team with a small budget," Claudine Snape from Asthma UK told us, "we have to continually innovate to find new solutions. It's something we look for in new staff."

Although don't tell *that* to the board.

 We encourage innovation by welcoming new ideas or more efficient ways of doing things and regularly review successful projects by other charities that have tried new approaches. In our team meetings, we make an effort to create space for innovation by celebrating success and talking about things that didn't work so well and why. Our organisation's competency framework includes references to innovation which also helps to encourage staff.

Claudine Snape, Asthma UK

Innovation has become a real buzzword at Friends of the Earth, and it has a strong presence in our organisational strategy. We're encouraging people to be less risk averse, balancing this with the imperative to be cost efficient. There's a lot happening now. In the context of campaign development, there are new ideas being tested – for example, an education programme around environmental awareness. Our fundraising investment strategy focuses on diversification of the portfolio through developing and testing new products, and our digital team is developing new co-creation approaches with public supporters. We're trying to 'hardwire' innovation into our project teams, which helps us unearth new ideas from people who might otherwise not be heard.

Adeela Warley, Friends of the Earth

 ## CASE STUDY: **World Vision: Investing in innovation**

Steve Wood, head of marketing and campaigns, World Vision

Woody Allen is quoted as saying, "If you are not failing every now and again, it's a sign you are not doing anything very innovative."

It's hard to disagree with the sentiment of these words. However, for those of us working in this sector, we live with the additional weight of knowing that every pound which doesn't deliver a return could have been better used to change a life. Our job is to balance this with the knowledge that without people being prepared to fail, we'd still be living without text giving, midnight walks and a bunch of comedians getting together every other year to raise millions.

In response to an identifiable need for more of that entrepreneurial spirit, international children's charity World Vision invested in a permanent Product Innovation team for the first time in 2010. It's only a small team – two full-time roles – but is supported by additional resource around the UK organisation and its global partnership. Of course, this doesn't mean we don't expect every member of the World Vision team to approach their work with a desire to innovate, but the advantage of having a bespoke team is that they're paid to think that way.

If only it guaranteed success.

In 2009, World Vision UK began working on a new Microloans product. Not hugely dissimilar to the Kiva online lending site or a sister product launched around the same time by World Vision US, Microloans enabled donors to give someone in the developing world the opportunity to start a business and change their future. Three years later, in 2012, World Vision UK took the difficult decision to end its investment in the product, having failed to deliver the targets we'd set for ourselves.

Here are four key things we learned along the way:

1. **Make sure you have the right resources in the right places.** Having an innovation team is rarely enough. In the case of Microloans, we thought we'd cracked it because we had a dedicated resource. However, we hadn't taken full account of the additional support that would be required from our data, systems integration, digital, supporter care or finance teams. The result: additional pressure on already busy colleagues and unnecessary delays to the delivery schedule. So make sure you are aligned and supported, both strategically and tactically across the organisation. It will save you an awful lot of pain.

2. **Build in freedom and flexibility from the start.** Here's where it gets tough. True innovation needs space; it needs to be released from the constraints of your everyday business, including income targets. Having a stretching income target in the first year of a product's life cycle might focus the mind, but is also likely to stifle the creative, innovative thinking that's required if your new product is really going to set some fires burning. It was one of the issues faced on the Microloans project and, as a result, the behaviours it drove simply weren't consistent with great innovation.

To be clear, this doesn't mean we shouldn't have strong governance, key performance indicators and a clear stage-gate process. They are vital if we're to remain truly accountable to our donors. The key is a framework that facilitates freedom and doesn't remove it.

3. **Don't be afraid to steal**, especially if it's from somewhere else in your organisation. I've already made reference to the fact that the Microloans product was launched by World Vision US just before the team in the UK picked up the brief. You'd think that would have resulted in almost identical product offering. Unfortunately, we fell into the 'our market's just not the same' trap and developed a product

with a different proposition, different creative and a different infrastructure. Next time we'll be less precious. By all means tweak, but know when to be big enough to accept that someone else might have got it right.

4. **Know when to stop.** We got this one right. As much as we all feel a personal connection to the success or failure of a product or initiative because we know the difference it can make, as much as significant funds may have been invested in a project, it's sometimes the right decision to halt any further expenditure on something that simply isn't working. This was the case with Microloans.

Make no mistake, it will hurt. And you must – no excuses on this one – record and share what you've learned from the experience. If you catch yourself thinking you haven't got time to do this, just take a second to imagine explaining to a donor how you made the same mistake with the next product as well. That usually does the trick.

As I'm sure you may be thinking, none of this is rocket science, nor will it guarantee that every product is successful. However, if it highlights nothing else, it should remind us all of the importance of learning from our mistakes. Here at World Vision, I have no doubt that the success of a subsequent innovation – Raw Hope – is a direct result of our striving to improve on the experience with Microloans.

As another famous American, Abraham Lincoln, once said: "My great concern is not whether you have failed, but whether you are content with your failure."

The impact of digital

Digital communications can't really be called 'new media' any more, but only relatively recently has it moved from the fringes of non-profit communication to becoming truly central to how we do things. For many organisations, it's now the most important communication channel.

The timing is probably about right. Even though the internet has been part of our lives for a generation, it has only recently become a mainstream channel to rival television, radio and the press. At the time of writing, internet use in the UK stands at about 85%, with TV at 97% and newspaper readership at 70%. From broadsheets to tabloids, the circulation of national daily newspapers has halved pretty much across the board since 2000, with some of this decline explained by audiences' 'channel shift' to their online counterparts. Simultaneously, mainstream participation in social media, blogging and other user-generated content such as online review sites has now reached a critical mass, and has proved a game changer for non-profit communicators. One example is the rise of low-cost video transforming how stories can be told, moving from high-gloss advertising to mini-documentaries, think pieces, infographics, video blogging and more.

New skills for new channels

Another reason for the increased prominence of digital in communications strategies is the fact that charity web experts have started landing the top jobs. In the past, communications directors were recruited from press offices, marketing and campaign teams, but now we're seeing web managers promoted to senior management. The skills they bring and their instinct for creating rewarding and interactive user experiences have proved invaluable in the new environment.

At one level, digital is much like any other communications channel, so you have to consider all the things we have covered in this guide, such as objective, audience, message and so on. But on another level, digital communication is a very different beast, marking a major shift in terms of how it's changed our audiences' needs and expectations, as well as our organisations' capacity to meet them. As digital specialist, Justin Spooner, notes: "It would be useful to stop thinking about digital as a channel, and instead think about it as 'how we work these days', because it has changed fundamentally how organisations function, far beyond the web team."

> When I started out in communications, I could write a press release then give the key messages to the CEO, who would do the interviews and that would be the end of it. That linear approach to communications doesn't exist anymore. The model is changing and so are expectations. Communications have become more personal and less corporate. It's not about broadcast any more; it's about recommendation and sharing.
>
> **Ben Hewitt, Save the Children International**

Audience expectations

Internet communications have changed what audiences expect from charities, not just in how they engage online, but across the board. People now demand much greater transparency and responsiveness, which is a truly fundamental challenge that many charities still struggle with. Audiences now want more authentic and personal relationships with non-profits. You can't behave as a faceless corporate entity and you cannot ignore people, since they are now using your channels to communicate with you publicly. So you must engage as human beings. You will need to consider what this means for your organisation because it does carry risks, but also huge opportunities if you genuinely embrace personalised, two-way communications through online channels.

This expectation of a more personal, less corporate voice applies right across your communications mix – not just online. It's interesting that the Edelman Trust Barometer (an annual survey of who people trust for information) has shown a surge in trust for individuals over organisations. They want to hear from your policy experts or your chief executive more than from your organisation or a nameless 'spokesperson'. This change must surely have been driven by the informal nature of web communications and the increased visibility of individuals within organisations. People, not organisations, communicate online, and our audiences seem to like that.

The centre of everything

Increasingly, digital has become the centrepiece of communications projects – even those that are led through other channels, whether in earned or bought media. Whatever you are doing, audiences will expect your website and social channels to be the main place to transact and communicate with you, as well as the place to find your organisation's definitive position. So it's important to fully integrate digital into any communications programme from the very start and ensure coherence of message across your channels, as well as provide the means to interact with you.

New ways of working

Every team in your organisation has a stake in digital communications – or should have. This is no longer the sole remit of the web team.

Organisations that succeed in digital communications have recognised this and established new ways of working. They have embedded digital skills and capacity across other teams, among press officers, fundraisers, campaigners and so on. Technology has become so cheap and accessible that you have to expect everyone in the organisation to be using it to communicate in some form. This in itself has become a resource that you should carefully consider as part of your strategy.

Now, digital teams are increasingly becoming the people who promote digital literacy and who help and train others to use digital in their own disciplines. Just as the team that manages the telephone system doesn't make all the phone calls, the web team remain the experts and manage quality, but are not necessarily the gatekeepers or 'channel owners'.

Keeping it purposeful

You shouldn't be afraid of letting your colleagues use social media to talk about your organisation and your issues (chances are they're going to, whether you like it or not) but there are some risks attached. Many people have become very confident in using digital communications and you may find some of your most unlikely colleagues are prolific social networkers. They could be a great resource to mobilise with a little careful management.

To make it all work effectively, it should be possible to create policies and guidelines for social media use, to manage messages carefully and help your organisation 'stick to the script' without curtailing free and fluid engagement. Some of the communications heads we spoke to give their colleagues regular tips and suggestions about what to include in their social media posts, saying that a more enabling 'Here's what you can do' approach has worked a lot better than a proscriptive one.

As you mobilise your colleagues, you should introduce the idea of genuine and useful engagement with social media users. One hundred people taking an e-action will usually be more valuable than one hundred likes on Facebook, so while general buzz is good for building online relationships, from time to time you will want to direct your online networks to do something for you. So, as in any communications channel, remind people to think about the purpose of their social media activity. What are you having this conversation for? To raise money? Influence policy? Promote services? Ultimately, digital communications should translate into something happening in the real world – otherwise it's just pixels on a screen. It's easy to forget that.

A place for listening

Another great benefit of digital communications is that it can enable much deeper engagement with your audiences and provide you with very quick insight into what they are thinking and talking about.

> We used to run a lot of focus groups to help us learn from our audiences, which are expensive. But now they tell us what they think on Twitter. That dialogue doesn't dictate our corporate messages but it gives us great insight, and if there's a serious mismatch then we know there's something wrong with our strategy.

Hilary Cross, Macmillan Cancer Support

Social media gives your audiences a voice, which can be a great resource for organisations that can mobilise them around their cause. But it can also pose a risk as negative remarks are often accepted unchecked and can spread like wildfire, causing reputational damage regardless of their factual basis. Few non-profit organisations face a daily battle with their public reputation but they do need to be prepared to respond and engage quickly when challenges come up. And so listening to the conversations can help you learn a lot, both good and bad.

Despite these opportunities, the people we spoke to felt there are still few non-profit organisations using social media really effectively and that there is currently too much fixation on counting 'likes' and 'follows' without enough thought about the depth of that engagement and the real value to the organisation. Social media is yet to prove itself as a serious fundraising channel, yet its power to reach audiences quickly at low cost and as an influencing space for opinion leaders and key journalists is undeniable, and it should have a presence in just about any communications strategy.

CharityComms' *Guide to social media for charities* goes into more depth on these issues.

Digital has moved very centre stage in our communications thinking. Because we have a small digital team, we have to think about what its role is and what the organisation's role is in exploiting digital channels.

We're trying to create online tools that can be repurposed for more than one campaign and we're getting the team to 'skill up' the wider organisation, allowing others to have a voice. So now our policy experts are using popular channels such as blogs, Facebook and Twitter. As long as you put good practice guidelines in place, our approach is to enable all of these people to be heard, rather than create bottlenecks.

Adeela Warley, Friends of the Earth

CASE STUDY: Cancer Research UK: Responding to media changes

Nicola Dodd, head of PR and social media, Cancer Research UK

Whether you are campaigning for change, defending your position or trying to get the public involved with a fundraising campaign, without the right relationships and a well thought-through story or comment, you are going to struggle to achieve any sort of cut-through.

And despite the fact that the way we contact the media has changed significantly, the key ingredients of great content and great relationships still stand true. In fact, they have never been more important.

So what *has* changed in charity PR?

The big changes are that 'media' can now mean anything from a broadsheet to a blogger and anyone's opinion on your brand can become visible (or even viral) very quickly. Also, engaging people with your story is about tailored content, not just a press release. And if you are not thinking digital, then you need to rethink your approach quickly because PR campaigns increasingly rely on content that people want to talk about and share online.

PR professionals have always known how important story-driven content is, and now there are even more opportunities to use this type of content to achieve our broader comms objectives. But the lines between who earns, owns and buys media are more blurred than ever, so we need to work collaboratively with our colleagues in other marketing disciplines.

It goes without saying that social media has become an important part of PR. It's a way to engage directly with our audiences and hold conversations without relying on press releases. But it's really important that it's used strategically and that we work with digital colleagues to get the most out of it. There's no point having a Facebook page if you don't know what you are trying to achieve or how it aligns with your PR and communications objectives.

At Cancer Research UK, we jointly own the social media strategy with our digital colleagues. This means that our journalistic, news-driven approach to content, through a social media hub in the PR team, works hard organically, but we use our digital colleagues' expertise (and sometimes budget) to extend its reach.

Thinking digital and social doesn't mean that we should stop thinking about print and broadcast media. There's still nothing like a *Today* programme interview to set the news agenda, 'getting a celebrity on the sofa' to talk about a campaign or getting a front-page national newspaper story. And contrary to popular belief, I don't believe the death of the press release is imminent, especially not for news stories. It might be accompanied by an infographic and sent as email copy, but at the end of the day, it's still a press release.

Of course there are challenges. We all know someone who still thinks a piece in print in the *Daily Mail* is more influential than a piece on *Mail Online*, and would never be convinced that the right blogger could have more influence than either. And depending on the size of charity you work for, you may have to prioritise a different part of the communications mix to deliver your objectives.

But media fragmentation doesn't mean an approach to PR that's about quantity over quality, digital over print or expensive multimedia content over press releases. Instead it's about taking those key ingredients, content and relationships, and approaching them in a targeted way, with a firm grip on how they work together in the current fragmented media landscape.

Approaching PR in this way should make us more creative and more effective in helping our organisations achieve their often life-changing objectives. It also puts the skills we have at the heart of our campaigns while allowing us to collaborate and learn new skills from other communications colleagues.

Action points from Chapter 7

- Start with an open mind, and be media neutral – understand which channels your audiences are using before deciding how to reach them.

- Different channels do different things, so be mindful of what you want to achieve when choosing your channel mix.

- Digital channels have transformed the relationships you can have with your audiences, so discover how you can use them to best effect and avoid potential risks.

- Make it matter and be clear about your goals.

8

Making the case for investment

At some stage in the development of your strategy, it is likely that you will need to ask for investment, either from the board or from your executive team.

We have made this the last chapter of this guide because it follows a logical flow. That is, decide what you need to do then try to find investment to do it. However, in practice, this is just as likely to happen right at the start of the strategy development process or midway through, depending on your organisation's budget cycles and the timing of your board meetings. If this happens to you, don't panic. It may feel back to front but it needn't cause you too much difficulty, and there are obvious advantages in knowing what investment is available before you produce your strategy.

Whichever situation you find yourself in, the principles for asking your board for money remain the same.

Rule number one: know your board

Whatever happens in your budget round, probably the single biggest factor in whether you succeed in winning investment from your board will be how well you've understood their needs and expectations. Just like any of your audiences, your board members will be motivated by a range of different propositions, and the more you understand what they are, the less chance you will have of a nasty surprise when you put your investment case in front of them.

So take the time to talk to board members as you develop the strategy, perhaps involving one or two in the process, and take guidance from them on what the rest of the board will be looking for. If you can't get direct access to the board, ask your chief executive to sound them out and get a steer on what they are expecting to see from you. You could also produce an early, interim paper for the board, signalling your direction of travel, priming them for the big reveal. If there's one thing boards don't like, it's a surprise. That's understandable – it's their job to be cautious. So if your strategy includes any radical changes in direction, you must warm the board up along the way or risk triggering their almost instinctive resistance.

It's all about knowing who's making the decision – what sort of person they are. Are they analytical? Would they be swayed by the financial argument? The threat to the organisation of not doing the work? Do you need case study examples? Examples of a competitor doing the work? Cost/benefit analysis? These are the different tactics I use depending on who's making the decision. Experience has shown that you might have the best case in the world, but fail to win people over because they're motivated by other things. There's nothing worse than knowing that you have a strong case but haven't managed to persuade the board because you've not taken all of this into account.

Richard Davidson, Anthony Nolan

Show some efficiencies

If you are asking for investment, remember that they have heard it before. After all, how often does someone submit a new strategy to the board without a price tag? So it's always a good idea to demonstrate that you aim to fund your strategy not only through new investment, but also through making savings and efficiencies in your current activity – for example, cancelling or slimming down certain projects or reviewing suppliers and finding cost efficiencies there.

Include Big Tactics

Remember: most people don't think about communications from a strategic point of view and your board is no exception. Just because we're telling you in this book that raising awareness for its own sake may be pointless, or insisting you make sure your social media strategy is properly targeted, it doesn't mean your board members think this way too. Some will look at communications from a very tactical perspective, zooming into specifics such as which celebrities you plan to recruit or whether you are going to rebuild the website.

But if your strategy includes examples of the major pieces of activity you want to invest in – your Big Tactics – you will help your board understand the overall strategy better, because you have given them a tangible illustration of what it looks like in practice. They will also be able to see where the money's going.

Make the right case for your board

In our conversations with communications heads while writing this guide, we asked them how they had gone about winning investment in communications strategies. The answers they gave fell into two basic categories:

- Communications can help achieve our business aims.

- Our brand has inherent value and we must invest to maintain or grow it.

Furthermore, either of these can be argued both positively and negatively, and some people we spoke to told us that simply painting a picture of a dreadful world without a communications strategy did the trick. So this gives us a third category:

- The risks of underinvestment.

The case you make will depend largely on what you know about your board and what's going to motivate them. Let's explore these positions.

Communications to achieve our business aims

If you have been through a rigorous process where you considered fully how communications will help achieve organisational aims, it follows that you should be able to make a strong case for your strategy.

In our Homes for Youth example, our communications strategy was built around three organisational objectives.

Taking the first of these – increasing voluntary income – the case could be made on the basis that strengthening brand preference will improve fundraising performance over time. The link between brand strength and income is notoriously difficult to quantify, but it's possible to show correlations by looking at how other brands have performed in the same sector, narrowed perhaps to UK housing and related social causes. If Homes for Youth researched its market during the discovery phase, it should have some data to help make this case.

Looking at the second Homes for Youth objective – increasing young people's access to support services – it should be possible to build a strong case on the basis of value for money. It should be straightforward to show that the charity will reach far more beneficiaries through targeted mass communications than through direct referrals alone. It could add to this the wider benefit that mass communications will serve a useful and secondary function in informing a large number of young people of their housing rights, regardless of whether they access its services directly.

The last objective is about establishing housing for young people as a political priority, which is probably the toughest one to put a price tag on. However, it should be self-evident that news media and popular opinion play a pivotal role in shaping the public agenda, and so if the organisation is committed to this objective, the board should expect to invest in communications to achieve it.

Brand value

A business case built on brand value, or brand equity, argues that the brand is an organisational asset with a real financial value that needs to be protected or grown. The concept of brand equity is by its nature intangible, so it can be difficult to get to grips with. Think about it like this: if the entire world suddenly ceased to recognise the Coca-Cola brand overnight, how many fewer bottles and cans would it sell? The difference between the profit made by the unknown Coca-Cola and the known Coca-Cola is the 'brand equity', because that difference is derived solely from the value (equity) of the brand.

Let's imagine a parallel in the charity sector. If two charities ran identical direct marketing campaigns, but Charity A was very well-known (or preferred) by its target audience, and Charity B was not known at all, you would expect Charity A to perform significantly better. Again, that difference is brand equity.

> Ask your director of finance what the benefit of a strong brand will be; she or he may come up with some great ideas and even help you figure out its value to the organisation. Ask them to set out the risks of not having strong communications and use this to build a consensus around what you want from your communications strategy.
>
> **Ben Hewitt, Save the Children International**

Of course, the trouble with brand equity is that even though it's undeniably real, it's very difficult to quantify. There is one very famous international brand company that places specific financial value on brands by using a complicated formula that basically subtracts all of a company's tangible assets (buildings, computers etc) and its measurable intangible assets (knowledge, skills, etc) from the company's overall value. What's left is an evaluation of brand equity. However, the problem is that the consultancy fees for making this evaluation can run into six figures, which would almost certainly be better spent delivering your communications programme.

But for all its complexity, you can use the principles of brand equity to make a much simpler case. For example, you could argue that because a sizable proportion of your voluntary income depends on having a strong brand, a small percentage of voluntary income should be reinvested into brand building in order to maintain or grow income. Let's set that at 2%. If you are a £30m charity, that equates to a communications budget of £600,000.

One contributor told us, "I wanted to manage the board's expectation, so didn't want to promise that investing in the brand would guarantee more money. Instead, I argued that it would lead to more opportunity.

And I made the case that if this wasn't done, it would result in loss of income, profile and opportunities, and we'd get left behind."

In this context, 'opportunity' is used to describe brand equity. And they were right about guaranteeing more money. Promising an attributable return on investment for communications activity is best avoided, since that pushes you into much narrower activity where communications is only valued as an instrument of fundraising. Thinking about brand equity should help you talk about the value of your work without having to over-promise or guarantee immediate results.

Risks of underinvestment

Some people we spoke with have made the case on the basis of a more negative framing – that is, highlighting the risks of not having a communications strategy with adequate investment. As a rule, we would avoid using this approach on its own, as it can put you in the difficult position of appearing to hold your organisation to ransom. But risk should certainly be part of the picture. If in the course of your strategy development you have identified genuine and significant risks to your organisation, then it is your duty to bring them to the attention of senior management or the board. So try to take a formal and measured approach to reporting risks, and neither underplay nor exaggerate them. These risks may come in different forms, including:

- **Risk of failing to achieve organisational aims.** This is just a negative spin on the first investment case we looked at. If communications investment will help achieve organisational aims, then it follows that underinvestment risks failing to achieve them.

- **Risk to income.** Again, the flipside of the argument that investment in brand building is good for raising money.

- **Risk to beneficiaries.** This may apply, for example, to charities that provide information and advice services to beneficiaries. Limiting or withdrawing such services could pose a risk to the welfare of the people that depend on them.

- **Reputational risk.** Arguably, having capacity in both press and social media is an important mitigation against attack from journalists or members of the public. For many charities, this is a relatively low risk, but for those working for controversial causes or campaigning in a hostile environment, the risk can be very significant.

- **Risk to the wellbeing of staff.** In some circumstances, you may find that staff are overstretched to the extent that it has become a serious issue, and that investment is needed simply to make their work manageable. Bear in mind, however, that if you are the communications head your first role is to manage workload and you would be expected to show that you had done all you can to reduce the pressure on your team.

 ## CASE STUDY: Prostate Cancer UK: The case for investment

Vivienne Francis, director of communications (acting), Prostate Cancer UK

Back in 2011, alongside a major rebrand (including a name change to Prostate Cancer UK), the board agreed an unprecedented level of expenditure in a mass communications campaign.

Identifying the business problem

The first step in persuading the board of the business case for this level of investment was to identify the business problem. The new brand needed to be a platform to publicise the issues surrounding prostate cancer and to grow the charity's market share in terms of 'helping more men' and 'raising more money'.

Setting priorities

Together, the senior management team redefined the three simple priorities for the organisation to focus on in the short and longer term:

- Support men – by providing excellent specialist services and driving others (for example, relevant healthcare professionals) to change their approaches appropriately.

- Find answers – through massively increased investment in ground-breaking scientific research.

- Lead change – making prostate cancer the big issue it deserves to be and changing behaviour, whether on the part of GPs and secondary clinicians, men at risk, or new and bigger donors.

Marketing and communications must have an impact, directly or indirectly, on the first two priorities. However, this could only happen if there was sufficient investment to affect the third. To organise our thinking, we defined a simple two-tier marketing strategy to:

- Build penetration of men with the prostate cancer gene (grow market share) by engaging healthcare professionals to 'nudge' patients to come to us.

- Generate significant and profitable charity-owned income by building salience of the cause and the charity's centrality to it.

These two tiers would be mutually supportive:

- Reaching and helping more diagnosed men will increase the propensity of many to make their own donations to the charity, donations we otherwise would not get.

- Stimulating more people to donate will increase the likelihood of more diagnosed men coming to us for support.

Reaching key audiences

We identified our key audiences as 4,000 secondary healthcare professionals and around 75,000 GPs and practice nurses who we would engage to 'nudge' a much higher percentage of the 250,000 men living with the disease to come to us. However, success in our pursuit of the second tier of our marketing strategy would require significantly higher investment to create compelling communications and reach enough people to make a difference.

The purpose of the 'Sledgehammer Fund', our multi-channel campaign, was to wake people up to the issue of prostate cancer and recognise our need to raise funds to support more men and search for answers. We therefore had to be truly ambitious with our creativity in order to cut through and 'stick' in people's minds. We also needed to 'box clever' to find additional ways to reach our audiences over and above traditional media.

A very real objective was to achieve media presence and impact three or four times the financial cost of the media we bought. We therefore looked at what the big health/age charities spend on consistent advertising. The data strongly indicated that these organisations see a real need for and payback from consistent advertising investment in their brands.

Our intention was that our message, while being tailored for some, would have broad emotional resonance with our primary audiences – dads, wives, granddads, daughters, sons – and other highly relevant audiences who need to see that we're out there and mean business – doctors, nurses, politicians, corporate decision makers, journalists, potential volunteers, potential support group members, etc.

The media investment underpinned our fundraising strategy. We undertook to review the performance and contribution of our communications on a consistent basis, with baseline metrics, targets and measurement systems put in place and a recognition that we would be accountable for the growth to which we were committing.

Fuelling growth

Awareness of the adverts we created was very high, around 48% in the general population, with prompted awareness of the charity's brand remaining constant at around 30%. It was 7% before both initiatives. There has been a steady increase in demand for our services and more income. New partners, such as ITV and Deloitte, tell us that the new brand and campaign made us more attractive as a prospect, and the campaign turned up the volume on the disease, making it a cause to 'be a part of'. It's an investment that will also play a crucial role in doubling our charity-owned income over the course of the next three years.

Ultimately, we're creating a movement for men, an idea of solidarity. Results so far suggest that we're already making headway with this.

Action points from Chapter 8

- Make sure you know your board, and their expectations.

- Consider which case you will make to the board: based on organisational objectives, brand equity, and/or risk mitigation.

- Share some of your 'big tactics' with the board, to help visualise the strategy.

- Show some efficiencies too.

Making it matter:
final thoughts

By now, you should know what developing a communications strategy entails and what creating communications that really matter, that make people engage with you and choose you, means. As you embark on that process yourself (a process that can be uniquely rewarding both organisationally and personally), don't forget to refer back to this guide and take, adapt or remould any and all of the advice you find here.

As our contributors have shown, there are certain tasks, tests and tenets that are central to all good communications strategies. But ultimately, every strategy is, by definition, different, and what really matters is that the strategy you implement is shaped by the objectives you set for yourself at the outset. It succeeds or fails by those standards alone, and if you have done it right, that success can be transformative.

It's a process that requires commitment, insight and, often, courage. But it's a process that could revolutionise the way your organisation goes about its work and the positive impact that has on the world around you. Good luck and do let us know how you get on.

Communications strategy template – skeleton draft

Introduction
What a communications strategy is, why this organisation needs one, and the difference it will make. The general approach we aim to take, and the scope and duration of the strategy. How this strategy was developed.

Setting the context
A narrative articulating the current 'state of the world' for our service users, our supporters and our organisation. Performance to date of our communications function. Benchmarking against others. Challenges we anticipate over the strategy period.

Organisational objectives
What our organisation aims to achieve over the strategy period (taken directly from the organisational strategy, if there is one).

The function of communications
A narrative articulating the potential role of communications in achieving this organisation's objectives, and the benefit of communications recognised as a central strategic function.

Communication objectives
What, specifically, this communication strategy aims to achieve. Includes complementary objectives across other departments, where relevant.

Audiences
Audience insights and segmentations, explaining who we aim to communicate with, what we know about them, what they want from us, and what we want them to think, feel and do.

Our brand
How we aim to position the organisation and the role of our brand in achieving organisational aims. How we will demonstrate impact of our brand. Brand goals and metrics.

Key messages
Matrices of key messages by audience and/or objective, supported by proof points.

Key channels
Outline of which channels will be used to reach each audience. Narrative explaining in broad terms how these channels will be used.

Big tactics
The major pieces of tactical activity we'll use to deliver the strategic aims.

The case for investment
The investments that will be required to deliver this strategy, and the benefit they will bring.

Appendices
More detailed documents to support the strategy, for example audience segmentation data, or analysis on media performance to date.

Resources

Chapter 4

'Defining mass-market audiences'

TGI (Target Group Index) - http://www.kantarmedia.com/product/tgi-surveys

MOSAIC - http://www.experian.co.uk/marketing-services/products/mosaic-uk.html

ACORN - http://acorn.caci.co.uk/

Office of National Statistics - http://www.statistics.gov.uk

'A few frameworks'

The Common Cause Project - http://valuesandframes.org/

Cultural Dynamics Strategy & Marketing - http://www.cultdyn.co.uk/

Mindspace - http://www.instituteforgovernment.org.uk/publications/mindspace

Chapter 5

'Do you have a brand strategy?'

CharityComms' Best Practice Guide, *Branding Inside Out* - http://www.charitycomms.org.uk/articles/branding-inside-out-a-best-practice-guide

Chapter 6

Show and Tell: a Best Practice Guide to portraying beneficiaries and service users - http://www.charitycomms.org.uk/articles/show-and-tell-our-first-best-practice-guide--2

Pitch Perfect: linking voice and values - http://www.charitycomms.org.uk/articles/pitch-perfect-linking-voice-and-values

'What words should we use?'

Plain English Campaign - http://www.plainenglish.co.uk/free-guides

Chapter 7

'Media analysis and planning tools'

The National Readership Survey - http://www.nrs.co.uk/

Ofcom - http://www.ofcom.org.uk/

Office for National Statistics - http://www.statistics.gov.uk/

Alexa.com - http://www.alexa.com/

Comscore - http://www.comscore.com/

Sprout Social - http://sproutsocial.com/

Google alerts - http://www.google.co.uk/alerts

British Film Institute research and statistics unit - http://industry.bfi.org.uk/rsu

'Audience expectations'

Edelman Trust Barometer - http://www.edelman.com/insights/intellectual-property/trust-2013/

'A place for listening'

CharityComms guide to Social Media for Charities - http://www.charitycomms.org.uk/articles/charitycomms-guide-to-social-media-for-charities

Thanks to our contributors

This book has benefited from the invaluable help of many people who have contributed their ideas, shared their experiences, commented on drafts or proof-read copy. We'd particularly like to thank:

Adeela Warley, Friends of the Earth; Andrew McLaughlin and Daniel Dodd, National Trust; Ann-Mari Freebairn, SSAFA; Athena Lamnisos, Community Links; Ben Hewitt, Save the Children International; Claudine Snape, Asthma UK; Elena Blackmore, Public Interest Research Centre (PIRC); Emma Harrison, VSO; Emma Taggart, Lullaby Trust; Frances Ellery; Helen Marsden, Marie Stopes International; Hilary Cross, Macmillan Cancer Support; James Renwick; Jessica Smith, Poached Creative; Jim Godfrey; John Grounds, RSPCA; Justin Spooner, Unthinkable Consulting; Karen Rothwell, RSPB; Laura Doughty, Stonewall; Lorraine Clifton and Liz North, CLIC Sargent; Mathurot Chuladul, Making Music; Mike Lawrence, Eden Stanley, Mike Taylor, Mikeemedia; Nathalie Bowley; Nicola Dodd, Cancer Research UK; Polly Markandya, Médecins sans Frontières; Richard Davidson, Anthony Nolan; Ruth Richards, Mind; Sam Upton; Selena Chapman, Marie Curie; Steven Buckley, Christian Aid; Steve Wood, World Vision; Tamara Bennett and Nick Radmore, BHF; Victoria Shooter, National Deaf Children's Society; Vivienne Francis, Prostate Cancer UK; Zoe Amar; Zoë Camper, Arthritis Research UK.

Index